D0206235

Semantics
and
Communication

Semantics
and
Communication

third edition

WITHDRAWN

NOV 17

SAINT LOUIS UNIVERSITY

John C. Condon, Jr.

University of New Mexico

P
90
.C64
1985

Macmillan Publishing Company
New York

Collier Macmillan Publishers
London

Copyright © 1985, John C. Condon, Jr.

Printed in the United States of America

All rights reserved. No part of this book may be reproduced or transmitted, in any form or by any means, electronic or mechanical, including photocopying, recording, or any information storage and retrieval system, without permission in writing from the Publisher.

copyright © 1966, 1975
by John C. Condon, Jr.

Macmillan Publishing Company
866 Third Avenue, New York, New York 10022

Collier Macmillan Canada, Inc.

Library of Congress Cataloging in Publication Data

Condon, John C.
  Semantics and communication.

  Bibliography: p.
  Includes index.
  1. Communication.   2. Interpersonal relations.
3. Semantics.   I. Title.
P90.C64   1985   001.54   84-3966
ISBN 0-02-324200-0

Printing: 1 2 3 4 5 6 7 8   Year: 5 6 7 8 9 0 1 2 3

ISBN 0-02-324200-0

To My Mother and Father

———————

Preface

In revising *Semantics and Communication* for the third edition, I often thought of my father's remark about remodeling an old house—that it sometimes seems easier to build from the beginning than to try to work around what has already been constructed. But since my father, who is in his eighties, is still building or altering something or other, it is clear that the exercise provides its own pleasures.

The pleasure of revising a book that will soon enter its twentieth year in print are many, not the least of which is the satisfaction of having survived that long. But there is more. Though *General Semantics* has had its ups and downs as an approach to communication, the underlying assumptions and goals are, if anything, as strong now as they were forty years ago.

Whether our society is any more sensible or careful about its language habits than it was a generation ago is hard to say. Clearly, some things have changed, and for the better. I believe that the often unwitting sexist bias in much of our language has been reduced considerably, and as a result, we have all been made more careful about the words we use.

. Not all indications that our language habits provide demonstrate such an improvement. The semantics of nuclear weaponry, for instance, seem to have changed very little in twenty or thirty years, despite the incredible advancements in the technology of destruction and despite the apparent progress in our own awareness of this grave threat. Curiously, these most destructive of human interventions can be "useful" to mankind only as symbols.

Both social attitudes and language regarding some "taboo" topics have changed dramatically over the past twenty years, and as usual, it is not always easy to say how one influenced the other. In this edition, we take up the issue of taboo, topics and euphemisms. There is a brief consideration of three basic tabooed areas: death, certain bodily functions, and sex. Also, we look at two other topics for which people are still trying to find the "right words"—handicapped and elderly people.

Also new to the third edition of *Semantics and Communication* is an exploration of creativity and problem solving in terms of semantics. Language habits can dull our thinking or help us to be far more imaginative. I have included a number of exercises and problems throughout the text which readers can play with individually, or better still, can discuss with others in class. This edition also expands the discussion of interpersonal communication by introducing notions of context and the reciprocal influence of messages and the interpersonal relationships between those who exchange them.

Examples and particular topics change over the years, but the underlying issues in semantics and communication remain the same. Social critics say that our society has entered into an era that stresses *information processing* and the providing of services. Interpersonal relationships are, if anything, more abstract than ever before, personal communications are conducted by technologies for transmitting symbols that are so complex we can scarcely understand. My modem can talk to your modem! But somewhere down the line we must translate symbols, whether they are words on a page or signals bounced off a satellite, into something that is meaningful to human beings. The power we have given to symbols has never been greater. And so, too, the need to understand certain basic things about semantics and communication has never been more crucial.

I would like to thank some of the people who have given me support and encouragement for a long time: Lloyd Chilton, my always cheerful and remarkably patient editor at Macmillan; Arthur Hastings, who encouraged this book in the first place; my colleagues, who recommended improvements for this edition; and Ken Frandsen, who brought me back into a semantics class in the enchanted land of this country.

J.C.
Albuquerque, NM
1984

Contents

Contents

Contents

Semantics
and
Communication

———————

1

Introduction
To An Attitude

It is conventional to begin a textbook with a brief definition of its subject matter. A book on semantics, however, might begin by asking the reader what *semantics* means. This is not a rhetorical question. Nor is the author being coy or pleading ignorance. If you answer the question honestly, you are already on your way to understanding what this book is all about.

Suppose, for example, you are taking a course in semantics or one that talks about semantics. Then your response might be something like this: "*Semantics* is the word used by people who can't agree on anything and so they agree they are having problems with semantics." Or: "*Semantics* is a word in the course in which we talk about words." Or even: "*Semantics* is the name of the course in which I don't understand what's going on." All these responses are relevant to the question (though they may not be acceptable for some instructors' examinations—so you should be careful what you underline in this book) because all are responses to the word *semantics*. And the study of semantics is the study of how people respond to words and other symbols.

Now, perhaps you have just underlined the previous sentence, in which case *semantics* means, in part, that particular response. By the time you complete the book, with several yards of underlined (literally or mentally) phrases, the subject will have come to produce some change in attitude, be it to boredom or ecstasy (hopefully neither). The subject here is not so much a catalog of definitions and observations as it is an attitude toward language, reality, and human behavior. And this is another reason why it is unwise to begin the book with a concise definition: to do so would miss the point. To paraphrase what somebody once replied when asked, "What is Zen Buddhism?"—first of all, it is not answering a question like that!

We might do better to indicate what the subject is *not*, because the word *semantics* is used in many ways in conversation and can be confusing. Like its older cousin, *rhetoric*, the word *semantics* is often used pejoratively, referring to verbal nuances or hair-splitting distinctions. "Look, let's not get hung up on semantics"; or, "It was nothing, only a semantic problem." Such remarks are not uncommon. But, as we shall see shortly, calling something "a mere semantic problem" is itself another kind of semantic problem: that label often means "trivial problem," or "irrelevant," and hence one that might be ignored. Obviously, the kinds of semantic problems in which we will be interested are not best regarded as trivial or irrelevant.

The term *semantics*, used more seriously, identifies the study of meanings."[1] And yet there are many approaches to "meaning," not all of which are relevant to our interests. Some scholars trace the historical development of words (etymology); scholars in linguistics study the diffusion or spread of words over a social and

---

[1] Usually, this refers to the study of meanings of *words*, and less often the meanings of other conventional symbols (religious symbols, coats-of-arms, flags). There are also special names for each of these studies, however. In recent years the semantics of nonverbal expressions has attracted greater interest. Because of the limitations of the scope of this book, however, our concern will be primarily with the verbal level, usually within the range of single words to phrases, not smaller units such as phonemes or larger units such as essays, speeches, or novels.

geographical area, noting regional differences. Such studies are often quite interesting and informative, even helpful—so long as one does not conclude from them what a word *should* mean.

Semantics and Semiotics

Years ago, Charles Morris proposed a new discipline that would be a general study of symbolic behavior called *semiotics*.[2] He divided the subject into three parts. One of these he called *semantics*, or the study of the relationship between words (and other symbols) and what these words represent. For example, the word *book* represents the thing at which you are looking. A second part of semiotics was *syntactics*, or the study of the relationship between words and other words, symbols and other symbols. Syntactics thus includes grammar, syntax, logic—in short, all rules of symbol systems. Such rules make "This is a book." one kind of statement, "Is this a book?" another kind, and "a this book is" a garbled group of words. The third part of the subject matter he called *pragmatics*, the study of the relationships between words (and other symbols) and human behavior, including the way words and other symbols influence how we act. Today *semantics* is popularly used to mean more or less what Morris described, the study of symbols and their referents. But that is not exactly what *this* book is about.

Our interest leads us to a more *general* semantics, one that does not look only at words and things but at the human behavior that results from using symbols in particular ways. In terms of Morris' definition of semiotics, we are equally concerned with the pragmatic as well as the semantic aspect of symbols. Indeed, we may argue that one cannot tell the meaning of most words without observing how the word is used, and what effect it seems to have on our behavior.

[2]Charles Morris *Signs, Language and Behavior* (Englewood Cliffs, N.J.: Prentice-Hall, 1946).

3

This makes our interest considerably different from that of most linguists, who usually are content to examine the syntactic dimension of languages, language as a system unto itself. And until recently, most linguists were reluctant to approach even the narrower view of semantics, for such study took them outside the system and into "reality." Perhaps the closest most linguists have come to this interest has been in hybrid disciplines such as socio-linguistics, ethno-linguistics, or psycho-linguistics.

Alfred Korzybski (1877–1950), who coined the term *general semantics*, was as much concerned with philosophy and psychology as with "mere words." Educated in the sciences and engineering, Korzybski was impressed with the precision of the language of science and the need for symbols to match an objective, empirical reality. Consequently, he was dismayed by the language of politics and diplomacy which he encountered when he served as a translator for the League of Nations just after World War I.

Korzybski believed that language influenced not only thinking, but all of human behavior. The effect, he felt, was part of our nervous systems. Thus, if our language habits were immature or distorted, our behavior would also be immature or distorted. Indeed, most of human behavior, from Korzybski's point of view, was "unsane." He sought to achieve a universal therapy through the linguistic retraining of human nervous systems. The title of his major work, *Science and Sanity*, states his concern rather clearly.[3] (Unfortunately, the rest of the book is not so clear.)

Like John Dewey and other writers of that period, Korzybski held high ideals and proposed an ambitious program to change fundamentally certain ways of thinking which he felt were inadequate for the modern era.

Some day behavioral semantics may pass into another field, perhaps psycho-linguistics, perhaps semiotics, perhaps some as yet undeveloped discipline that will fully incorporate studies of nonverbal languages—music, film, art, or whatever—with the

[3]*Science and Sanity*, Second Edition (Lakeville, Conn.: The International Non-Aristotelian Library, 1947).

traditional concern with words. In the meantime, semantics takes its place among the behavioral sciences which attempt to explain why we behave as we do, be it wisely or foolishly, sanely or "unsanely."

It is during college, perhaps for the first time, that we become acutely conscious of language and communication, and hence of semantics. As a student you may feel that you are among an elite of the curious and intelligent, qualities that are both verbally based. From the library to the dorm, yours is very much a world of words. You take seriously some of the noises made by the professor or by your roommate (and more seriously still, the sound of your own voice). You agonize over scratches on paper, called themes or term projects or examinations, and submit them knowing they will return with still more scratches—which you may take still more seriously.

You explore the world with pen and book, and you carry home verbal treasures with which you enhance your writings and utterances. You may find it increasingly difficult to talk without seeming to sound like you've been to college.

You are asked questions you had never thought about before and formulate answers that seem impressive. You discuss the nature of human nature. Maybe you distinguish between "internalization" and an "external locus of control," and having learned to make such a distinction begin to question why you believe the way you do. You talk with others about the nature of "truth," about "alternate states of consciousness," or about distinguishing "a good writer" from "a great writer."

You discuss until you are bored or amused by the answers or lack of them, but you discuss. You formulate an answer but it does not sound quite as profound as the answer by Plato or Kierkegaard. You comfort yourself by knowing that you are in good company. In your waking life, and even during some of your sleep, the verbal activity is constant.

This book is written with the modest hope that if you can understand your language habits and communication processes a little better, all this verbal activity may be a little more significant.

5

Our Symbol-laden Culture

Millions of Americans begin their day something like this: A radio alarm clock awakens them, perhaps with music, and later with news. They dress according to the fashion and what the weather report recommends; they listen to the news of prison riots, of wars in far-off lands, or sports scores from across the nation. A famous man has died, and the millions are saddened, if only briefly. They may gobble down a vitamin pill but then skip breakfast, quickly brush their teeth, and hurry off to work. If they drive, they watch their speedometer to stay under the legal limit while keeping track of how much time they still have to arrive at their destination on time. This is how the day begins.

For a day to commence (and continue) in this manner these millions must have accepted a very sophisticated and complex set of symbols, for there is very little in the description that is not heavily endowed with symbols. The *clock* that wakes one—a revolutionary change from not so many centuries ago, when the sunrise or a rooster did the job with the result that days varied considerably from season to season. With the invention of the clock, the abstract notion of time was arbitrarily marked off into convenient units. The choice of *clothing*—formal or casual, coat and tie for men, heels for women, how many buttons on the coat, how wide the tie, how high the heels—is arbitrary and quite unrelated to the more practical purpose of keeping the body comfortable. This is not to say that style means nothing to these millions, for the hyperbolic teenager "would rather *die* than be caught in last year's style!" The *news reports* that enrage or sadden the millions are of people they have never met, of events they can never know, of places they have never been. Nevertheless, for these millions the names on the news *mean* more than the names of their neighbors. The *vitamin pill* appears to be like thousands of other pills, but the label on the bottle is impressive: "percentage of RDA: Thiamine mononitrate—5,000 percent, Ri-

6

boflavin—4,410 percent, Pyridoxine Hyrochloride 3,750 percent
. . . ." They compulsively brush their teeth, because they believe
that brushing prevents cavities (though most do not really know
why). Their wallets and purses are filled with other symbols: credit
cards and what Marshall McLuhan called "the poor man's credit
card," money, licenses, and identification cards without which,
in a symbol-laden culture, they may be unable to prove who they
are. They drive on the right side of the street because they agreed
to do so. They agree to travel at a speed beneath that seen on
traffic signs and assume that their speed is correct when a needle
on the dashboard points to the appropriate number. And the
millions hurry to their destinations because they have agreed to
begin work at nine, and being too early will communicate something undesirable to their colleagues (and themselves, perhaps)
and being too late will communicate something else to their
bosses. Out of respect for the millions, we will end the story
before the day's *work* begins.

The history of human civilization is a history of the increasing
importance of the symbolic dimension of life. By and large, increased industrialization brings with it additional systems of symbols. We have to learn many languages we do not even recognize
as such; humankind lives not by words alone. Susanne Langer
has said that "the symbol-making function is one of man's primary
activities, like eating, looking, or moving about."[4] We might add
that our symbols dominate other primary activities: what, when,
and how much we eat; what we see and do not see; and how
and where we move about.

What we learn to classify as *edible* is largely determined by
cultural considerations, and what makes the mouth water in one
place seems to turn the stomach in another. Few Americans long
for snake, cow's blood, or sheep's eye, but these are delicacies
elsewhere. The thought of breakfasting on food usually classified
as dinner fare is enough to upset the stomach's of some people.

---

[4]Susanne Langer, *Philosophy in a New Key* (Cambridge, M.: Harvard University
Press, 1942), p. 41.

In a similar way, virtually every act apart from some involuntary physiological responses is bound up with a larger symbolic system. Of all such systems, language is by far the most important.

Of Mice and Monkeys and Men— Signs and Symbols

More than a century ago, Charles Darwin presented an idea in *The Origin of the Species* which continues to guide our thinking: that the behavior of every species has a survival function. When the survival mechanism fails, the creature will cease to exist. What the bee or beaver needed to survive in 2000 BC is pretty much the same as what the bee or beaver will need in 2000 AD. But if conditions of the environment had changed enough during those four thousand years, the bee and beaver would have joined the brontosaurus as extinct species. The skill for survival is built into all life, a literal and complete "design for living."

Darwin's thesis should hold for humans as well as any other form of life. Yet human beings are different. Humans have developed a physiology slightly different from even our nearest simian cousin. We possess a forebrain (cortex) that is larger than the closest ape, and this distinction, which is one of degree, permits us a behavior which appears to be utterly different in kind. With the enlarged forebrain, human beings can perform an exercise more marvelous than any of the animals we sometimes praise: human beings are able to think. As W. Grey Walter put it some years ago, physiologically[5]:

> Man ... is specifically what he is by virtue of thought, and owes his survival in the struggle for existence to the development of that supreme function of the brain. He is sapiens,

[5]W. Grey Walter, *The Living Brain*, (New York, N.Y.: W.W. Norton, 1953), p. 15.

the thinking species of the genus homo. The discerning, discreet and judicious one, even if he does not always live up to all these meanings of the name he has given himself.

From the time Darwin presented his evolutionary thesis, arguments have been fought about the relationship between humans and animals. More than half a century ago, at the famous Scopes trial in Tennessee, public attention in the United States focused on this issue, which pitted Christian fundamentalism against evolutionary theory and questioned whether it was legal to teach evolution in a high school biology class. Now, sixty years later, people still debate that issue.

People who otherwise hold the scientific method in high esteem can become upset when it is suggested that chimpanzees might be able to learn to use language in a sophisticated way. If you are ever at a dinner party and want to liven up the conversation, simply suggest that animals have a language ability that is comparable to that of human beings. When such claims are put forth in scholarly journals, the letters in response—both pro and con—are passionate.

Why? What is it about language as it distinguishes humans from lower forms of life that arouses such strong feelings? First, there is a Western tradition, encompassing religious, philosophical and even most scientific writings, that clearly regards human beings superior to animals. This is said to be due largely to our ability to use symbols, the result of our enlarged forebrain. If it should be shown that chimpanzees or dolphins are as capable as we are at "thinking"—meaning rational, reflective thought—then everything that has seemed "human" may be called into question. Consequently a long tradition and many widespread habits (such as eating meat and keeping pets) may be shaken.

The argument among scientists, however, is rarely expressed along these lines. Instead, the argument is in terms of a particular experiment, alternative interpretations of findings, weaknesses in methodology, and so on. In recent years there have been several attempts to teach language to animals, and in each case the results have been disputed and the implications challenged.

9

Herbert Terrace of Columbia University taught a chimpanzee, Nim Chimpsky,[6] well over one hundred signs (using hand signing, similar to signs used by the hearing impaired). Consider the following conversation:

Teacher: *What want you?*
Student: *Eat more apple.*
Teacher: *Who want eat more apple?*
Student: *Me. Nim eat more apple.*
Teacher: *What color apple?*
Student: *Apple red.*
Teacher: *What you more eat?*
Student: *Banana, raisin.*

The teacher is one of the trainers of Nin, the famous chimpanzee, and the student is, of course, Nim himself. Both are communicating not with spoken words but with signs similar to those used in American Sign Language.[7]

Koko, a gorilla trained by Francine Patterson at Stanford University, learned more than six hundred signs. Alex, an African gray parrot studying at Purdue University, has a vocabulary of more than forty words, which in itself is not unusual for a parrot. But Alex quickly learned to ask for certain objects by shape, color, and material, so he can say such things as "three-cornered green paper". In his weekly "semantics tests," Alex usually scores more than 80 percent correct. Studies of language and communication patterns among porpoises, whales, and other mammals now are common. All of these become enbroiled in controversy whenever any results are announced that seem to challenge the conventional distinction between human beings and other creatures: the ability to learn and generate novel combinations of symbols that indicate abstract thought. Until recently, it was assumed that

---

[6]The name Nim Chimpsky is a play upon the name of one of America's foremost linguists of this century, Noam Chomsky.

[7]Herbert S. Terrace, Nim: A *Chimpanzee who Learned Sign Language* (New York, N.Y.: Washington Square Press, 1981).

animal language was limited to patterns of what we have called signs. Now some people are not so sure.

But only some. Many are as sure as ever that the new behavior is only a more impressive repetoire of signs. Others say it is truly symbolic behavior. The controversy is likely to continue for quite some time. Unless or until there is some breakthrough, the conventional distinction between the symbol-making/symbol-using human and the sign-using animal will have to remain in place, albeit in a much less secure place. The crucial difference is one of abstraction: a rat may learn to find its way through a maze by trial and error, but it cannot plan the trip by studying a map. Or, as S.I. Hayakawa used to say, "You can teach a dog to respond appropriately to the words 'Hamburger now!' but not to the words 'Hamburger next Tuesday.'"

In terms of survival, the human ability to think means many things. It means, first of all, that people can adapt to a new environment; ultimately it means helping to shape that environment as well. The ability to think means also that only people can acquire skills with which they were not born. It is true that man was not made to fly, but in two generations, human beings have become the most skillful fliers known. The ability to think means that to a great extent humans can create their environment; only human beings can now live comfortably at any point on the earth, or under the seas, or even in space.

Unfortunately, along with these marvelous achievements come blunders and stupidity and cruelty that are unknown even to a rat. For though humans can turn the desert into a garden, can plan their community, and increase lifespan, only humans can also plan their deaths or the death of entire species. And no white rat would flee its property because a black rat had moved into the hole next door.

The ability to use language means the ability to transfer something of experience into symbols and *through the symbolic medium to share experience.* Through our ability to use language, we are capable of learning from the past. The human species thus has advanced while other creatures have not, cannot. Because human experience is built upon experience, change accelerates

11

at a geometric rate. Witness the developments in the past fifty years as compared to the previous fifteen hundred. As we have entered the "age of the computer," the promises for man are almost incredible. Never before has the retrieval and analysis of information been possible with the speed or accuracy permitted by this cybernetic revolution. To transfer the symbolic experience into meaningful human behavior is, of course, another task.

To review briefly, the human being is distinguished physiologically from animals by an enlarged forebrain or cortex that makes language and thought possible. Through language humans can express experience in symbols, and through those symbols can share experiences with other humans. The sharing of meaningful experiences results in the change we call learning. As we learn we advance, or at least change, from generation to generation. Animals, which are capable of communicating in varied but comparatively limited ways, cannot learn from each other, cannot change, cannot advance, at least not to the extent that man does.

The distinction between humans and animals finds its counterpart in the kinds of communication performed by each. Animals can learn to respond to signs, but it seems that only human beings can use symbols effectively. Susanne Langer expresses the difference by saying that signs announce but symbols remind. That is, animals can emit and receive cries signifying food or sex or danger. But an animal cannot contemplate the nature of food and thereby decide it might be a good idea to go on a diet.

One distinction between sign and symbol is the difference in the number of possible responses to each. A sign stands in a one-to-one relationship to an experience (or object or the like); a symbol suggests many possible responses. A sign of danger, such as a loud noise, may stimulate an animal to flee or hide. But the symbol of danger to man may mean many things, of which fleeing might be the least useful. It is easy to think of signs which man has devised, but it is difficult to find them used only as signs. Take, for example, the loud noise of a car honking. In some situations the honking may mean "get out of the way"—but it probably is more symbolic than that. The person honked at may have to consider whether the driver is indicating "get out of my way," "hello, it's me," "just married," or "we're number one!" Signs devised by people tend to become symbolic. A siren intended to signal the end of a class or a day's work invariably evokes other responses regarding obligations, relaxation, or even confirmation of the time by a glance at a watch. For animals, responses are much more restricted. Man may consider appropriate responses before acting. To jump at every warning is to put man at the level of the rabbit.

Mark Twain once made this same observation when he noted that we sometimes behave like animals instead of behaving like people:

> We should be careful to get out of an experience only the wisdom that is in it—and stop there; lest we be like the cat that sits down on a hot stove lid. She will never sit down on a hot stove lid again, and that is well; but also she will never sit down on a cold one anymore.[8]

To go from cat to mouse, we may recall Wendell Johnson's remark on this distinction: "To a mouse, cheese is cheese; that's why mousetraps work."

The more restrictive a society is, perhaps, the greater the emphasis on signs. The military, for example, may impose rigid standards for behavior that some would call *signal reactions*. ("If it moves, salute it!") Also, in times of stress, we often respond to a word (symbol) as if it were a sign: we react signally.

Ask yourself what are the words that are likely to set you off? What words seem to trigger a reflex reaction, often unrelated to the intent of the speaker? For many people "cuss words" provoke reactions that are largely beyond one's control. "Fightin'

---

[8]Bernard DeVoto (ed.), *The Portable Mark Twain* (New York: Viking, 1946), p. 563

13

words"—signs of bigotry, for example—may produce such re-actions. Sometimes, of course, the speaker is aware of the likely reaction and utters the taunts precisely with that intention.

Often, however, we respond signally without the speaker even being aware of how the words affect us. A particularly dramatic example was reported by a student during a discussion of signal reactions. The student would sometimes experienced epileptic seizures which seemed to be provoked by certain words. A speaker who might express how angry she was by saying "I nearly had a fit" could provoke a seizure, he said. Even the word *fit* in different contexts or in a form like *misfit* could signal a seizure. The student added that another kind of signal reaction could be observed in his class if he announced "I have epilepsy!"

For most of us, most of the time, our signal reactions are less apparent, though not uncommon. Whether we jump to con-clusions, refuse to listen to information because of its source ("don't believe anything *he* says!"), or blush at certain words, we are also responding signally. Such reactions fail to use the re-sources of language as they might best be used. Learning to use language intelligently begins by learning not to be used by lan-guage.

2

From Experience To Symbol

Most people don't think very much about language. True, we are sometimes self-conscious about our speech or occasionally unsure whether to use *is* or *are* in a sentence, but to the process of speaking and listening we seldom give much thought. We think using language is like breathing—natural, normal, pretty much the same for everybody, and notable only when we are having trouble doing it. We've long since forgotten the effort, the years spent and the growth experienced in learning to speak as we do. We overlook the fact that while the ability to use language is characteristic of human beings, each language, each dialect, and even the particular way of speaking for each person is unique.

We might do better to assume less about our language and about the meanings of words. We might want to be cautious about our assumptions. The assumption with which we begin this chapter may appear to be eminently sensible, even obvious. But by the conclusion of the chapter we will have reason to modify it as well.

We begin, tentatively, with the assumption that whatever

words might be considered, they are definitely something very different from the things they represent. Semantics usually begins with that assumption of duality. The distinction has usually been stated in the negative: "the word is not the thing." Linguists and psycholinguists are developing descriptions of the nature of *words*, whereas the philosophers formerly and the scientists currently have pursued the investigation of *things*. Studying the relationship between the two and emphasizing the importance of the distinction is the special province of the semanticists.

Sensible critics (including, perhaps, you) often have been puzzled by a discipline that emphasizes what appears to be so obvious. Who, after all, would assume that a word is the thing it symbolizes? The answer, semanticists reply, is written throughout history and through much of our daily lives, in which we seek after, purchase, love, fight, and sometimes die for words. As our culture becomes more symbol-laden, even symbol-bound, the recognition of that distinction becomes still more important.

The ability to symbolize means the ability to call up internal experiences, using only the symbols. Whether one is reading a novel or reading a grade on some term paper, the symbols stimulate some changes in the body chemistry. For example, if before retiring to bed, you read a ghost story, you may find it difficult to fall asleep immediately. You are not *really* afraid of ghosts, but your reactions to little marks on paper may affect your behavior in a way you cannot control. Or, if before retiring to bed, you read a textbook, you may find it difficult to stay awake. (Here, of course, we are not talking about the relative merits of ghosts and academics, but about one's attitude toward such symbols.) Or, to take one more common example from the classroom, you might consider the power of your instructor to affect your nervous system just by organizing three lines to form either an A or an F. What has caused the changes are clearly responses to *symbols*; such responses are sometimes called *semantic reactions*. For more dramatic examples, you might read the literature of psychosomatic medicine or note the "power of suggestion" that a hypnotists can exert on a subject.

16

Thus the semanticist is interested not only in *words* as they are different from *things*, but even more in the pervasive responses to symbols.

The World as Perceived

If you have ever flown in a plane, this recollection may be familiar to you: From the window you see below a landscape clear and ordered. Along the coast line, the waves press methodically. You can almost see their birth from a silent sea and their steady movement to the shore where they disappear. Each wave is separate. You can count them. Inland the pattern of traffic moves slowly, without noise, without confusion. There a bus moves out to pass a truck; there the cars slow at what must be a stoplight. The back yards of the houses are clearly marked, and in the distance the patches of farmland neatly mark their own borders.

The view is a pleasant one, but since you spend most of your time on the ground, you know that neither shoreline nor terrain is so ordered and so without movement and clash. You know that as your plane descends the world seems to speed up, the invisible becomes immediate, the silent becomes noise, and the few become innumerable. What had been a patch of green becomes a park of trees with shimmering leaves. What had been a steady glow of orange becomes a sputtering neon sign.

When you feet are firmly on the ground you realize you have not returned from illusion to reality. You have only returned to what is most familiar. If you had the proper apparatus you could descend still farther into a microscope world, as different from the familiar landscape as it had seemed when viewed from the plane.

The history of physics has been the history of this kind of descent into the stuff of the world, always seeking that ultimate

17

level beyond which there is no further change. As the exploration of the submicroscopic world progressed, physicists were forced to abandon what previous generations had thought was permanent: elements, then atoms, later electrons and protons, once believed to be the indestructible stuff of the world, successively failed the tests of permanence. Where has this exploration brought us today? And what does this have to do with semantics? Bertrand Russell describes both:

> Energy had to replace matter as what is permanent. But energy, unlike matter, is not a refinement of the common-sense notion of a "thing"; it is merely *a characteristic of physical processes.*[1]

What characterizes *reality* at all levels is not the presence of some *thing* but rather of a *process.* Rather than speak of the *things* of the world we should speak of the *events.*

Our language is a product of centuries, and most of our vocabulary reflects an older, prescientific view of the world. We retain a vocabulary suggestive of permanence when we know today that the only permanence *is* change. Metaphorically, we speak of the *things* of the world as if they were like rocks, when we know they are more like flames. What we once thought were like nouns now seem more like verbs. In the light of the discoveries of the past century, our vocabulary is peculiarly anachronistic. Of course, individually, we need not and certainly cannot easily change the structure of our language. But being aware that a nonverbal world of *process* is represented in words that indicate a *static* quality is important.

In one sense the essential awareness in the study of semantics is the awareness of what we cannot directly perceive, that world-in-flux. This is fundamental in the assumption that no words can ever accurately represent a *thing*, for things are dynamic and words are static. Of equal importance in a discussion

---

[1] Bertrand Russell, A *History of Western Philosophy* (New York: Simon and Schuster, 1945), p. 47. (Italics added.)

of things is the awareness of the process by which we apprehend the events of reality—perception. For just as there is much we are incapable of perceiving, there is much that we can perceive but characteristically do not.

The human perceptual apparatus is impressive, even if it cannot notice the continuous process in the world. Unaided, the eye can discriminate among an estimated seven million colors. It can see an object the size of a grapefruit at a distance of a quarter mile. But the perceptual apparatus is also misleading. It fools us into thinking that the moon grows smaller as it "rises" in the sky. (The distortion is largely the result of seeing the moon in the company of roofs and tree tops; one way to correct this distortion is to bend over and view the moon through your legs.) When still picture are flashed at the speed of sixteen per second, we see the pleasant illusion of a continuous natural motion on the screen. Knowing what produces the illusion does not make it any less effective.

Even our own faces are seen by us as optical illusions. How many times have you looked at your own face in a mirror? Would you say that the face you see reflected back is the same size as your own face, larger than life size, or smaller? You might be surprised. Next time you are in a steamy bathroom with a mirror, trace the outline of your face on the mirror; then measure it and compare it with your actual face size. You may be surprised to find the image is much smaller than the size of your actual face.

It is the brain no less than the eyes that is the principal organ of sight. At a quarter of a mile we can see a telephone wire that few camera lenses could record even under ideal conditions. What we are able to do that the camera cannot is to construct the wire mentally from only a few visual cues.

Even the "blind spot" located near the retina of the human eye does not usually prevent us from seeing what it obscures. Discovered three hundred years ago, the blind spot actually obscures an area eleven times the size of the moon when we are looking into the sky. Instead, our brain fills in what is blocked by extending the surrounding environment into the blind space.

It may be said that everything we see is an optical illusion that is the result of our expectations, our training, our values, our goals. Like the familiar optical illusions that appear in children's magic books and Sunday newspaper supplements, what we see depends on how we look at it and who it is that is doing the looking.

What we see (or hear, smell, feel, and so on) depends on what we think we want and need to see. And this in turn depends on who and where we have been and who we think we will become. Perception is an active process, not something natural or identical for all people with comparable eyesight. The human being seems to need to be selective of all of the possible stimuli. We need to organize the stimuli, to disregard the apparently irrelevant (and sometimes the threatening), and to make sense out of the stimuli we do perceive. If we were sensitive to the billions of stimuli that bombard us each second, we would be rendered incapable of doing anything. (Pause from your reading for a second and look carefully at this page—see all of the tiny pits and marks on the paper that you had not noticed; perhaps you can observe delicate shadings in the paper of colors you had not seen before, colors that are especially difficult to point out verbally. Now listen carefully for sounds you had not noticed before.) If the nonfunctional marks on the paper or the irrelevant sounds were important to us, we could learn to perceive them— but we could not notice all the marks and still concentrate on reading the page, or hear all the sounds and still follow a serious conversation. We must be aware that we are constantly being selective, and that what we do perceive is but the tiniest part of what is perceptible.

Gestalt psychologists have studied why we perceive as we do, emphasizing the need to organize the stimuli that meet the eye (and other sensory organs). We think we see the details of a familiar face in a newspaper photograph, but on closer examination we can see that there are only tiny dots, regularly spaced but of various sizes, which produce the apparent blacks, whites, and shades of gray. There is no *face* on the page; there are only stimuli that *we can organize* into a face. We *create* what we

20

see around us to a degree much greater than is commonly recognized.

We see mostly what we have learned to look at. We look at what we think we *need* to look at. We ignore what seems unnecessary or, in some cases, what seems threatening. However, we are *sensitive* to far more stimuli than we may realize.

An experiment was conducted in which picture were flashed on a screen at such a rate that those watching could not be sure what they were seeing. Instruments were set up to record eye movements during the process. Even though the subjects in the experiment were not consciously aware of what they were seeing, the pupils of their eyes contracted when the pictures were distasteful or threatening. "Neutral pictures" produced no such responses.[2] The point would be missed if we thought this perceptual phenomenon occurs only in the laboratory. Such unconscious avoidance of personal danger is a part of our everyday behavior.

A similar experiment testing one's ability to recognize words flashed on the screen for a very short time indicated that individuals characteristically see words that are consistent with their personal values and misread words that are irrelevant or opposed to their value systems. For example, one subject who had ranked low in the aesthetic area of a standard value test misread the word *elegant* as *hyprocrisy*.[3]

The same principle has been used—or abused—by some advertisers to introduce words just below the threshold of consciousness in order to affect the responses of consumers. *Subliminal* messages may be embedded in photos or drawings; the word *sex* for instance, may be suggested by the contours of ice cubes in a glass in a liquor advertisement. The efficacy, no less than the ethics, of subliminal advertising has been disputed for many years, but there is sufficient research to demonstrate that

[2]Eckhard H. Hess and James Polt, "Pupil Size as Related to Interest Value of Visual Stimuli," *Science*, 132 (1960), pp. 349–350.

[3]Leo Postman, Jerome S. Bruner, and Elliott McGinnies, "Personal Values As Selective Factors in Perception," *Journal of Abnormal and Social Psychology* 43 (April, 1948), pp. 142–154.

the words that evoke semantic reactions can be presented even without our being aware of their existence.

One's culture as well as one's personal background also influences perception. In another experiment, people from the United States and from Mexico viewed pairs of pictures through a stereopticon of the sort usually used to create the illusion of three-dimensionality. In this case, however, the two pictures were completely different. One represented a scene from Mexico (a bull fight, for example), the other a scene from the United States (a football game, for example). Several sets were shown to both groups. Those from the United States consistently "saw" the football game, the Mexicans "saw" only the bullfight.

If you have traveled in another country whose language you did not know, perhaps the signs you noticed most were the ubiquitous ads for Coca-Cola or other familiar products. Such ads do not really dominate the landscape of the world, but when we are given the set to see them they often seem to. We see what we have learned to see. We tend to listen more closely to songs we have heard before than to new melodies. We pay more attention to what is pleasing to us than to the unpleasant. We tend to pay more attention to a football game our team is winning than one our team is losing. We tend to prefer to hear the political candidates we favor and to read the magazines that reassure us of our social perceptions rather than those that show us another picture.

The effect of memory and expectations based on past experience is so strong that we frequently see things that are not really there and fail to see things that are there. Read the phrase in the triangle:

If you did not find an error, read it again and ask yourself why you did not see it. The explanation for this is the same explanation for the inability of some parents to notice their children growing up, or for some professors to fail to see a bias in their reasoning, and for most of us to see inconsistencies in our behavior.

This myopia increases when we are under stress or in conflict. Psychologists Albert Hastorf and Hadley Cantril have written a provocative (and yet familiar) description of what happens when the students and alumni of rival colleges watch a football game.[4] Their investigation showed the extent to which apparently sane, educated men and women are unable to agree on what has happened, even after the cheering has stopped and the event is viewed on film. Princeton fans saw dirty playing on the part of Dartmouth, with refereeing that was patently unfair. Dartmouth fans saw the same improper conduct, but to them it was obviously the fault of the Princeton eleven. Their analysis of a Dartmouth–Princeton football game led the investigators to a conclusion about perception that applies to all events. It is a conclusion, we might add, that is at the foundation of the semantic attitude:

> ... It is inaccurate and misleading to say that different people have different "attitudes" concerning the same "thing." For the "thing" simply is *not* the same for different people whether the "thing" is a football game, a presidential candidate, Communism, or spinach. We do not simply "react to" a happening or to some impingement from the environment in a determined way (except in behavior that has become reflexive or habitual). We behave according to what we bring to the occasion, and what each of us brings to the occasion is more or less unique. And except for these significances which we

[4]Albert H. Hastorf and Hadley Cantril, "They Saw a Game: A Case Study," *Journal of Abnormal and Social Psychology* 49 (January, 1954), pp. 129–134.

bring to the occasion, the happenings around us would be meaningless occurrences would be "inconsequential."[5]

A man trained in any profession or skill learns to see, to hear, to *sense*, what the unskilled cannot. Learning almost anything requires a change in sensitivity. As people are of different occupations and possess different skills and interests, perceptions vary accordingly. Even in areas where no special training is required, what one sees and what one is blind to depends on his interest and background.

The young mother learns to her the sound of her baby crying, although visitors to her home hear nothing. From the subtlest clues, one can perceive if something is troubling a close friend or mate.

Without training we may not be aware that we are not perceiving what the trained person perceives. In learning a foreign language, for example, careful training is necessary to *hear*, not to mention imitate, new sounds. To the Spanish speaker who is learning English, the English *yes* and his or her "zhess" sound alike, just as when we learn Spanish his or her *mesa* and our "maysuh" sound alike to us.

What all this means is that not only do we fail to see with anything resembling ideal objectivity," but we constantly rehearse our own peculiar perceptions. We enjoy becoming experts at being ourselves. And as we gather with like-minded (not to say right-minded) individuals, we give ourselves support that the way look at the world must be correct—for, after all, everybody else we know and respect sees pretty much the same thing. Our perceptions are most clearly limited and guided when the reality is social, when we look at the political, racial, economic, and moral pictures. Ask yourself how many friends you have who see a world different from yours. Ask yourself what books or magazines you read that show a world different from what you believe exists. In the broadest sense, perception of the world has less to do with

[5]Ibid., p. 133.

the sensory organs of the physical body than it does with the social body.

Abstracting

General semanticists have used the word *abstract* as an active verb to describe the process of perception. Abstracting involves three related phenomena: *ignoring* much of the stimuli that might be perceived; *focusing* on a limited amount of that stimuli; and, often *combining or rearranging* what is perceived to fit into some pattern that is particularly meaningful to the perceiver. These same three aspects of perception also characterize other aspects of our behavior. When we try to remember something, for example, we usually can recall only a small portion of what we had known or experienced; most is forgotten as we give emphasis to only a small part of what we experienced, and part of what we recall is likely to be a rearrangement of what was originally perceived. Also, when we pass along information to another person, some loss and some distortion is almost inevitable, following the same pattern just described. All that we can know is known through this active process. And all that we know is therefore a distortion of what is "real." This should not cause alarm when you think about it. But if you think about it, it should encourage a more cautious, less dogmatic attitude about knowledge.

The simple notion of abstracting is extremely important. For one thing, it suggests that we will have trouble comparing words or other symbols with some objective "reality." *Reality is practically, what we have already abstracted.* Edmund Leach, a leading British cultural anthropologist, makes a similar point in speaking of man's relationship to his culture:

> Travellers have often remarked of Australian aborigines that they seem to "read the desert like a book," and this is a very literal truth. Such knowledge is not carried in any man's head, it is in the environment. The environment is not a natural

thing; it is a set of interrelated percepts, a product of culture. It yields food to the aborigine but none to the white traveller because the former perceives food where the latter sees only inedible insects.

The bewilderment of many "ordinary" men in the environment of modern science is very similar. The environment is meaningless because we do not understand the code which would give perceptual order to our mechanical desert.[6]

In school one of the most obvious procedures of abstracting is taking notes in a classroom. It must be very uncommon for any two students to take exactly the same notes of a lecture. Sitting in different parts of the classroom probably has some influence on what is heard in the first place, and different guesses about what might be asked on an examination and different attitudes about exams, also will have an effect. Personal fatigue, interest in the subject, familiarity with the teacher's methods of lecturing, and much more come into play. The teacher says: "Although you won't be tested on this you should know something about Aristotle. He was born in 384 BC in the little town of Stagira on the eastern coast of the peninsula of Chalcidice in Thrace, the son of a court physician, Nicomachus." One student writes: "Aristotle—born 384 BC" Another writes: "Aristotle born on stagnant coast—son of a Greek physicist." Another writes: "Get tickets for the concert Saturday."

If this example seems too farfetched, arrange for everyone in a class one day to compare their notes. It may make one wonder about what is learned in class in which notes are taken. It certainly gives one pause when considering whose notes to borrow for a missed class!

Because we must abstract and organize only certain stimuli, it seems impossible to represent the world accurately in symbolic terms. We can become conscious of our abstracting, but being aware of our limitations is quite different from overcoming them.

[6]Edmund Leach, "Culture and Social Cohension: An Anthropologist's View," Gerald Holton (ed.), *Science and Culture* (Boston: Beacon Press, 1967), pp. 24–38.

Perhaps it is this awareness of possibilities and limitations that best describes what we call an *education*. It is an awareness, at least, that is basic to a study of semantics. Without it we might repeat the error characteristic of much of Western thought—to accept an *a priori* reality and set about to name the parts of it. Our assumption is that there is no *it*; that there are as many *its* as there are people at any given moment in history.

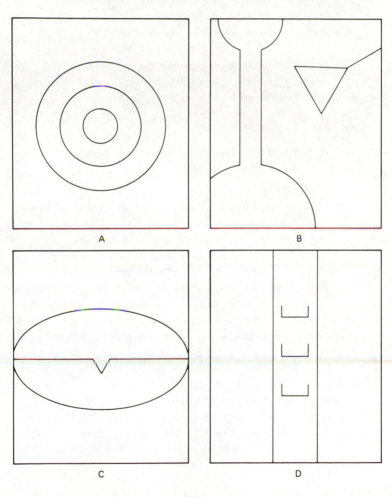

A

B

C

D

The Figure here depicts several hundred different pictures. At first it appears there are only four, but looks are deceiving. Look at picture A and name what you see—a bull's eye target? That is one picture. Some of the others include:

- A fried egg on a plate.
- A large pipe seen from one end.
- A detail of a crater on a topological map.
- A very heavy person wearing a straw hat.
- A melting marshmellow sundae

Question: To what extent do we see something and then give it a name? Another question: To what extent do we see something only after we are given its name?

A Second Look at that First Assumption

The distinction between the nonverbal (world of things, events, and so on) and the verbal, the object and its symbol, was the starting point for this brief examination of semantics. One cannot pursue the distinction very long before running into the problem of expressing "the thing," the nonverbal world, without the aid of language. In a book or lecture, of course, to designate any aspect of the nonverbal world requires a word, but the problem is not reduced when one does not speak or write but merely experiences or points at things. There is strong evidence that by the time we are conscious of perceiving or experiencing some sensation, we have already been influenced by the language and symbol systems we have learned.

If this seems to be true of the perception of sights and sounds in the outside world, it seems at least as true of internal sensations such as hunger or fear, to say nothing of more complex feelings such as love. Evidence for this point of view is substantial,

28

most notably in the work of Stanley Schacter.[7] It is Schacter's contention that there are two basic components that make up our emotions. One is physiological arousal. The other is the way we happen to label that arousal. In a number of extraordinary experiments, Schacter and his colleagues demonstrated that the way we *feel* an emotion, anger or elation, love or anxiety, depends mostly on how we label our feelings. That label is based on the way we *read* the environment around us.

[7]For a review of Schacter's theory and related studies, see Chris L. Kleinke, *Self-Perception; The Psychology of Personal Awareness* (San Francisco: W.H. Freeman, 1978).

3

Words, Words, Words ...

Learning the Language

The first breath of life is often noisy. This noise continues, except during rest, until the last breath, but the quality and purpose of human sounds undergo great changes, especially in the first two years. During these first twenty-four months the rudiments of a language are obtained. At three months the child begins a career of babbling, which usually reaches a peak in another four months. By the time the baby blows out its first birthday candle it is prepared to imitate adult noises. Within another half year it can utter several single-word sentences, and by the age of two the child's sentences include pronouns, articles, conjunctions, and prepositions. By the age of five the child knows the sound and structure of its language better than most foreign students with years of training, even if the child's vocabulary is less extensive.

How the child learns all of this is either clearly known or little known, depending on how specific an explanation one seeks.

Both babies and chimpanzees are vocally equipped to do the same thing, both are notorious mimics, but in the presence of adult speakers only the child learns a language. As discussed in the first chapter, the crucial difference between baby chimpanzee and baby *Homo sapiens* seems to reside in the larger cortex of the human infant. Nevertheless, it is imitation that elicits language. The few isolated (and unreliable) cases of infants that have survived away from human contact indicate that a child cannot teach itself to learn language or in any way "become human."

The child imitates what it sees and hears, without being aware of what all of this is about, and is rewarded when the imitation is a good one and is discouraged when the imitation is off the mark. If the child could utter an adult platitude in those early months it might say, "I don't know much about language, but I know what I like," for it is affectionate reinforcement it receives and not any conscious awareness of what it is doing that eventually produces language. The child learns by receiving a smile or a kiss or a spoonful of applesauce for saying *doggie* when one thing passes before it and saying *Daddy* when something else is there. At the outset the child knows nothing of strings of words or sentences; it merely imitates the sounds as best it can. To the young child, the sound of "kitty" and "look at kitty" differ only in difficulty of expression, not semantically. For this reason, children who for awhile may seem to understand certain words and phrases later prove to know only how to repeat them. A young child may seem to be able to correctly identify *Daddy* because the only adults he regularly sees are Daddy and Mommy. It comes as a surprise when the child begins to call the mailman and the meter reader *Daddy*, too. It is not that the child cannot distinguish his father from other male visitors, but rather that his verbal associations are too general. A noted writer tells of the time when he and his family lived near a park that featured an equestrian statue of General Grant. The statue was a favorite of his daughter, who was told that it was called *Grant*. Eventually it was necessary for the family to move elsewhere, and before leaving, the little girl asked her father if she could go to the park to say good-bye to Grant. This she did, saying "Good-bye, Grant, good-bye, Grant."

31

Later she asked her father, "Daddy, who was that soldier riding Grant?"

The process of learning to make socially meaningful noises and to interpret those of other speakers continues throughout life. The most basic vocabulary and structure is learned through repetition and reenforcement in the earliest years, so that it is unlikely that you can recall when you first learned to use most of the words you use every day. A vocabulary that is taught formally, with attention to definitions comes later. It is quite possible, for example, that you can remember when you first learned words such as *bifurcate* or *bauds*. Your associations with such words may include former school teachers, spelling contests, or browsings through an encyclopedia. Such words, unlike those of your basic vocabulary, are perhaps more easily defined than used. From the point of view of semantics, usage and meaning are ultimately difficult to distinguish, but in the process of growing up and learning a language the distinction is apparent.

It should be pointed out that the process of learning a language *for a child* is the same everywhere, for every language. No one's first language is harder or easier to learn than any other. The age and sequence of language learning is the same everywhere. Even if children have some illness that retards their language learning, once their problem is corrected they proceed along the same pattern, for this process, it now seems clear, is biologically based. (At puberty, however, the brain, as well as the more visible parts of the body, undergoes a significant change; one effect of that change is to make future language learning, such as studying a foreign language, both different and far more difficult.)

The work of Eric Lenneberg and Noam Chomsky has contributed greatly to our understanding of how a person comes to learn and use language. The thrust of both scholars has been to emphasize the universality of language: Lenneberg, in terms of physiology and biology, and Chomsky, the noted linguist, in terms of underlying structures of language. In the past it had been thought that we learned our language solely through imitation, what Roger Brown has called "the original word game," played between adults and children.[1] Obviously imitation is crucial—we learn the language spoken by our parents or those around us and not any other language. However, it has become clear that what we say, even as children, is not limited to mere imitation; we make all kinds of sentences that we have never heard. So it seems that a more accurate view of language learning is that we learn *principles* from which we *generate* new, often unique, utterances.

Those linguists who have followed Chomsky's thinking believe that the underlying principles of grammar are comparable in all languages. That is, although the surface expressions of a language may seem quite different, we have only to go beneath the surface to an underlying structure to find ways of transforming expressions of one language into expressions of another or to find the rules for generating unique utterances which are within our own language. Hence the name for this school, the transformational generative grammarians.

When my daughter was very little she once asked her mother, "Are you happy at me?" Apparently she had learned some rule based on "Are you angry at me?" and evolved a new expression. Chomsky, like most linguists, is primarily concerned with the *syntactic* aspect of language which we mentioned in Chapter 1. But the implications of his work might be significant for the pragmatic aspects which are the major concern of our study of semantics. If one is learning primarily learning principles, and if these underlying principles seem to be either similar or at least interchangeable in all languages all over the world, why should we assume that our language or language habits influence the way we think and act? This is a major issue and marks a departure from some of the basic assumptions of Korzybski many years ago.

That "original word game," establishes not only the basis for socialization, but also for all of thought and even much of perception. In some sense, then, children are partially correct when they believe as they do that people think with their mouths

---

[1] Roger Brown, *Words and Things* (Glencoe, Ill.:Free Press, 1958), pp. 194–228.

and ears.[2] By locating thinking in these areas, the child at least calls attention to the influence of langue on thought. To this extent the description may be preferable to the common belief of many adults in the existence of some organ called *the mind*.

Unaware of the influence of language andthe rather arbitrary way in which they have learned it, mature individuals may carry with them all their lives the patterns established in infancy. More committed to language habits than they are aware of and continuing to associate words and things, they may remain "infantile" in their thinking and behavior. It was such a position that Korzybski took when he developed his theory of a general semantics.[3] His assumptions of the child's language habits that remain influential in the adult's life are consistent with what others have discovered, and cannot be dismissed. And although our goal is not therapy, we will have occasion to return to these assumptions throughout the remainder of this book.

The First Dimension of Language

The Convention of Naming. The child learns that everything has a name and that these names must be very important to his parents because every time the child makes one kind of noise in association with a thing, his parents like it, and when he makes another kind of noise, they do not seem much impressed. This

---

[2]Jean Piaget, *The Child's Conception of the World* (Paterson, N.J.: Littlefield, Adams & Co., 1929, 1963), p. 38.

[3]The extent to which the general semantics of Korzybski was correct and useful or greatly exaggerated is yet to be determined. His ambition of a universal therapy through semantic awareness has not been realized, and his methods have been soundly criticized. One of the most intelligent criticisms of Korzybski, free of the polemics that have characterized so many writers in favor and against general semantics, appears in John Carroll's *The Study of Language* (Cambridge, Ma: Harvard Univ. Press, 1963), pp. 164–168.

training continues for years. Children love it because they are learning to do something very adult, and adults love it because they appear to be experts at it. The early rewards for correctly naming a thing are later replaced by other symbolic rewards— by gold stars in grade school, later by high marks, and eventually by certificates and diplomas of various kinds. Throughout life, being able to *name*—which is to say being able to make verbal distinctions that somebody regards as correct and important— is greatly admired. Naming may be *the* universal pastime. Naming is also the first dimension of language.

Naming is a convention. We should note right away that there is no necessary relationship between the sound of a word (or shape, if the word is printed) and what the word stands for.

There have been studies in phonetic symbolism which show that even in very different languages, given a pair of nonsense words and imaginary references to which to apply these words, people tend to agree on how to match the sound with the thing. All over the world, *gik* sounds like something lighter or smaller than *guk*, for example. And there is also the class of words called *onomatopoeia*, where the sound of the word is an attempt to imitate a natural sound. Attractive as this might seem, there are problems. For one thing our vocabulary tends to be much more visual than aural; we simply don't or can't conceptualize very much on the basis of sound. (What is the sound of a desk or a chair or a book?) Also, if we compare languages, we find that even the words that attempt to imitate sounds, such as dogs barking or bells ringing, are different in different languages. The words used to describe the sound of a dog barking in Greek is very close to the word used in English to describe a turkey gobbling.

If we desired, and everybody agreed to the change, we could call this book a *spaghetti* and could call spaghetti *book*. If the change were consistent, no confusion would result. Indeed, over many years the referents for certain sounds (words) do change, but because speakers learn the changes at the same time, there is no confusion. That the word *girl* once meant a young person of either sex or that the word *coast* was formerly applied to any border (Switzerland used to have a "coast") says something about the convention of naming and not about the history of girls, boys, and borders.

We make rapid symbolic changes all the time. For example, in playing card games the Queen of Spades "means" thirteen points in the game of hearts and ten points in blackjack. We don't argue about what the sound of *queen* really should mean; we simply agree to a meaning for the particular game and enjoy ourselves. It is this very flexibility that permits us to play so many games with only fifty-two cards. The same is true of the language game. So long as we are all playing by the same rules, using words in more or less the same ways, we can communicate reasonably well.

What we learn to call the things of this world is largely a result of our social and educational background. Whether you learn to *eat* dinner or *take* dinner says something about the social values your family has placed on these words. Whether you call a particular paper container a *bag* or a *sack* may depend on the part of the United States in which you have been reared (or *raised*).

Children who are instructed in what to call things and are corrected when they do not name objects in the same way that their parents do, often come to believe that there are correct names and incorrect names, and there is always just one to a customer. Perhaps the majority of children who ask "Why is the sun called the sun?" are told, "because that's what it is." (If they ask again, they may receive the same answer in a slightly louder voice.) Under such instruction the child's attitude can be understood. Without an awareness of the nature of his language the adult remains, in this sense, a child all of his life. One of the most common and most childish of adult arguments is the disagreement over what something should be called and what something *really* is.

In one sense, the parent is correct when he tells the child who asks why something is called what it is called, "because that's what it is called." (The adult should not say "because it *has* to be called that" or "because that is what it *is*," of course.) When one learns a language, whether it is his first or his second or tenth, it is not for him to ask *why* something is called what it is called. Etymology is a fascinating study, but it does not help one to speak a language or understand other speakers. Imitate others and play the word game. That is what we have all done, and that is basically what enables you to understand anything verbal, like this book.

Everything Has a Name.   The ability to give a name to everything often passes for education. It is a common belief that to be able to name something is to know it; to define something is to understand it. Neither assumption is correct, of course. There are dull and pedantic persons who have large vocabularies, and there are imaginative, perceptive individuals whose lexicon is limited. Despite such evidence, the belief that the more you can name the more you know persists. The explanation of language training and reward previously cited partially explain this.

The naming itself is not a problem, for naming is the basis of language. Rather, it is the erroneous attitudes about naming and the exaggerated influence of names that sometimes cause problems. Among the common mistaken attitudes abut names is that each *thing* has only one correct name. As indicated in the previous section, names are only matters of convention and convenience, and they change with the times. The one-thing/one-name assumption is not borne out.

Perhaps the most pervasive criticism of the obsession for naming that characterizes much of Western language and thought (based in culture, not language) is the need to know names in order to recognize experiences, and the corresponding attitude that experiences that are not named are irrelevant. How many persons can enjoy a fine piece of music without wishing to identify the composer and title? How many can enjoy the first balmy spring day without desiring to know the exact temperature? Or enjoy a piece of nonrepresentational art without knowing what it is called, even if the name is only ''Perspectives'' or ''Number 17''?

It is this exaggerated importance of naming every event, every experience, every thing perceived that is often disturbing. We seem most obsessed where the names and information are often

37

the least important, as in our statistical treatment of most sporting events. Few persons seem to realize that we could name as many things as we wanted. Like the specialist or hobbyist who, to the uninitiated, seems to talk in code, we could produce elaborate lists of names for *things* that have never been named. Such lists would be useless, of course, for the value of naming lies in its efficient notation of what is important and the way relationships can be indicated.

Once names are learned, at least two effects may result. One is the feedback effect on perception. *We begin to notice those things for which we have names.* Before taking a course in astronomy, you may have looked into the sky on a clear evening and seen only stars. After a few weeks of study you do not see *stars*—instead you see (or say you see) supernovae, white dwarfs, galaxies. Your responses to what you see may include a new and thrilling sense of distance and perspective, including a sense of your own insignificance in so vast a universe. Of course this results from knowing not just the names of the points of light in the sky but also how they are related and what you have learned about them. But such meanings must follow the symbolic distinctions among what had previously seemed to be "just stars." Thus, for better or for worse, when names are learned we see what we had not seen, for we know what to look for.

A second result of naming, which may at first appear to contradict the previous effect, is *the failure to see things once we have named them.* To take the previous example through another step, suppose we had never learned that those things in the sky were called stars because we had never bothered to look up at night. Then one clear summer's evening we cast our eyes upward and behold!—what do we see? It is possible that we will see only "stars," but it is also possible that we notice that the points of light up there do *not* all look alike. Lacking a single name for that range of brightness and color, we might notice differences and thus never assume they were all alike in the first place.

This seems paradoxical. In one case, learning names helps us to *see* what we had not noticed. In another case, learning names

Words, Words, Words ...

seems to blind us to what we would have seen if we hadn't learned the name. How can this be resolved?

Both possibilities exist in our behavior all the time. As we learn to name *things* we abstract certain characteristics in order to apply a single name to a variety of experiences, be they stars or breakfast foods. It would be impossible to have a language if every experience (defined in time and space) had to have a new name, and so we classify groups. In doing this we blind ourselves to the individual differences within the group. Later, as our education (and vocabulary) increase we begin to identify some of those differences. In many instances we notice so many differences within what we had previously considered one group that we no longer find the original single term very useful. This is exactly what happens when we pursue special interests. At the age of four all things that creep or crawl may have been identified for us as *bugs*. By the time we finish a biology unit in grade school the term *bugs* may not seem very convenient, and if we were to do graduate work in entomology the term *bugs* would be completely useless as a general term for insects.

It is impossible to know what distinctions a child makes before it learns language. William James' description of the infant's world as "One blooming, buzzing confusion" is as good a guess as any. This is usually taken to mean that the child has not learned to conceive of himself as a self apart from what surrounds him or to develop perfected perceptual skills for identification. It might also be interpreted as indicating the child is supersensitive to so many distinctions in the world about him that it cannot function, and that the first stages of language serve to dull this sensitivity and permit only socially meaningful distinctions to be made. Here we are in the realm of speculation, which is unnecessary to pursue further for our purposes.

This section may be summarized by noting that we learn to make verbal distinctions for the things around us. To the extent that our distinctions are gross, with many differences omitted, the process of naming may dull our sensitivities. To the extent that names remind us to look for distinctions we had not noted before learning the names, naming increases our sensitivity. When naming becomes so obsessive that we are discomforted when we cannot name an experience or when we think that a name is the most important characteristic of an experience, we are indeed confused. And so we are, most of us some of the time, confused.

The Elemental Problem.   Although elementalism in semantics may be regarded as an aspect of the previous section, it deserves special attention. By *elementalism* we mean the effect of arbitrarily imposing a static language on a process-reality that we experience. Elementalism calls attention to the linguistic division of the indivisible experiences of our lives.

As we begin to use words we begin to abstract *characteristics* from a single experience. If we take for an example one specific experience that might correspond to what we would label *a hot day*, our *experience* is not one of *hot* and another of *day*. *Our experience is one*—we could not have had *that* day without the *hot*, too. However, if language is to be efficient we must use relatively few words for an unlimited number of experiences, and so we distinguish our abstractions for use in many experiences. This is the convenience and necessity of language. What must be recognized is that only the *words* are repeated in other combinations, not the experiences. If this observation seems strange or confusing it may be that you have become so accustomed to your language that you assume that words must have a one-to-one correspondence to experience. You assume that if there is a word *hot* there must be *a discrete thing* that is hot, and so on.

Because our language requires us to organize our words in certain patterns as we would thread beads on a string or stack building blocks one on top of the other, we cannot avoid some form of elementalism. We can, however, be aware of what we are doing and know that this is a necessary evil of language and not a mirror of reality in our experience.

Part of the System.   The elementalistic problems of language that can more easily be attended to are those arbitrary divisions that may have once made sense but which, in the light of recent descriptions in science, no longer appear to. Einstein's contribution to semantics was an attack on the division between time and space. In some time in the future, we may no longer speak of the two as separate elements in our language. The traditional distinctions between mind and body, between ends and means, between material and spiritual, and so on, appear to be much weaker in this century than they have been traditionally. When the experiences they would describe are investigated carefully, the student finds that such distinctions are either meaningless or deceptive.

An important change occurred in the history of Western thought when philosophers and scientists stopped describing the world in terms of separate elements and began to describe relationships in process. The physicist stopped looking for an element called *heat* and began to study *thermodynamics*.

The approaches of transactional psychology, general systems theory, and other related fields which have attracted attention in recent years also reflect a shift from individual persons and things to relationships. Thus a therapist today may realize that a "problem child" in a family may only be a person identified as such by others; "the problem," however, may lie in the relationships between that person and the others in the family or, indeed, in a larger segment of society. Viewed in this way, the entire family may require counseling, not just the identified child. To effectively treat "alcoholism" or "hypertension" might require a kind of treatment for a whole network of social systems and behavior, for these problems are not individual problems that reside within people but manifestations of relationships at a level that is vast and complex. An increasing number of doctors today are viewing problems of "health" in this way.

"Health" as it is most frequently viewed in the United States today, and even as defined by the World Health Organization, appears as an ideal state that resides within an individual.[4] But,

---

[4] The World Health Organization defines health as "a state of complete physical, mental, and social well-being, and not merely the absence of disease or infirmity."

as critics have pointed out, not only is such an idealized state almost impossible to achieve or maintain, it is contingent upon relationships which are constantly changing. We may say that a person "has his health" in Chicago but that he "loses it" when he goes to the altitude of Denver or the heat of Arizona. We *can* talk about health that way, as if it were an "it" to be possessed or lost, but a more sensible description would be in terms of an individual's neurophysiological system in relation to his surroundings. "Health" is a limited description of an ever-changing process, not a *thing*.

Health provides an excellent example of the significance of our labels and attitudes. If health is some state that resides within a person, then in order *to improve* health we would probably want to assist that person. But if health is just the name we give to one kind f perception of a dynamic set of relationships, then we can affect a person's health at any number of points. At one level we might prescribe vitamins or medicine. But at another level, perhaps out attention should be directed at the person's living situation, family relationships, or neighborhood. Perhaps the problem is related to the individual's job, in which case we may see that the national economy and even international relations impinge on his or her health.

Such thinking is often part of policy making today. Do we reduce crime by hiring more police officers, or by providing better housing and job opportunities? Can we deal with such issues on the local level, or is it more appropriate to try to do something on a much larger scale? Some people respond that such large-scale responses are impersonal. Certainly this is often the case. However, to regard *health* or *crime* or *respect* as qualities that either do or do not reside within the individual is to do the reverse: to treat one expression of a dynamic social system as if it were a *thing*.

In our social relations, especially, the change from an elementalistic to a process attitude has been most important. The field of *group dynamics*, which reflects the attitude in its title, regards terms such as *leader*, *deviant member*, *true partner*, and *cohesiveness*, not as separate moving parts in a machine, but as in-

42

separable relationships of a group. In describing any conversation you cannot talk about one without talking about the others. If one member of a group is removed or another added, you do not just change the number of persons in the group, you change the nature and process of the whole group. In the home, if Grandma comes to live with the family, you do not just "add Grandma," you establish a new pattern of relationships. You no longer have the previous experience plus Grandma, you have something entirely new. Similarly, if a member of the family dies, you cannot just "subtract one"; obviously, there is an entirely new pattern of behavior to which you must adapt.

When one distorts his understanding of the process experience by regarding what words stand for as static elements that can be added or subtracted, he may also think of these elements as palpable things that have shape and substance. The child believes that one may touch thought.[5] The word *thought* fits into the same sentence patterns as nouns for material objects, and we retain, at least metaphorically, the idea of *thought* as a *thing* even as adults. (We will return to this theme in Chapter 4 when we look at metaphors.)

One interesting and significant treatment of process as elements is especially American and recent. This is our attitude toward time. Perhaps the vast majority of Americans believe that *time* consists of something they can save, waste, spend, keep, and so on. "If you save an hour today you will have it tomorrow," we may say. But one hour today is not the same hour tomorrow. Time at the age of twenty-one is not time after sixty-five.

In summary, we should note that the elementalistic bias is necessary in language, for words mark off arbitrary distinctions that do not exist in the reality they represent. However, when we fail to recognize this as a necessary evil of language and instead believe that reality is composed of elements that correspond to our vocabulary, we are abused by our language. What can be altered without altering the nature and structure of our language

[5]Jean Piaget, *The Child's Conception of the World* (Paterson, N.J.: Littlefield, Adams & Co., 1929), pp. 38–49.

are the gross dichotomies ("mind and body," and so on) that are neither consistent with contemporary knowledge nor particularly useful. We can also avoid describing our experiences in terms of simple mathematics, adding and subtracting attributes to or from a basic experience. All are parts of the whole, and to change any one changes all of the rest.

Language, Values, and Cultures

It is impossible to distinguish language fully from the cultural background and values of its speakers. Without some understanding of these values, we cannot appreciate the meanings of words as they are used in that culture. In the United States, for example, usually "yes" means yes, "no" means no. We value being blunt, practical, objective. In Japan, on the other hand, interpersonal relations are often more important than "objectivity," and indirection, vagueness, or ambiguity are far more valued than bluntness of speech. So in Japan you rarely hear the equivalent of "no," at least not if saying "no" might disappoint somebody. One student has catalogued at least eighteen ways of avoiding saying "no" directly, even though in most of these cases the listener fully understands that something like "no" is meant. And if it should come to a "yes or no" situation, some Japanese will switch into English to state such a crude choice.

Of course, no Japanese-English dictionary will explain this sort of thing; it is not a matter of simple semantics. Nor is there anything in the language, Japanese, English, or any other, which would account for this. We must look at the more general semantics of the culture, including the values which underlie and govern the use of expressions.

It has long been noted that what is valued in a culture or within a smaller group within a culture will be reflected in vocabulary. As a general rule the more words a language has for certain concepts, the more important are those concepts. Arabic used to have several thousand words to refer to the camel, but as the importance of the camel has waned, the word stock has also decreased. Where there are technological developments, inventions, and innovations, vocabulary is likely to reflect such developments. Consider the number of words we use for kinds of medicine or music or shoes or automobiles. Our vocabulary both reflects and directs our attention to making finer distinctions than other people make who have no such interest or knowledge. Slang and in-group speech is also an index of what is important. This kind of speech, characteristic of any subgroup, serves the members in two ways: it serves to symbolically distinguish the "in people" from the "out people," the people who talk like us from the people who talk like outsiders; and in that talking it serves to reinforce the interests and perceptions of reality that characterize the group. The same can be said for a culture as a whole. Virtually any identifiable group (cultural, regional, generational, etc.) will usually express its special character by ways of speaking no less than by ways of acting.

It is possible to distinguish one generation from another solely on the basis of speech, including as criteria not only what is talked about but which expressions are used. It is usually easier to identify some of the characteristics of other groups than it is to describe our own group (the others are the ones that sound funny). But if you could read transcripts of representative conversations from several different groups, you might well be able to identify many. Ways of speaking reveal distinct views of reality, and symbolic demarcations of what is valued. At the same time, ways of speaking evoke an identification with others as well.

If we extend our notion of languages to other nonverbal symbol systems, including hair style, dress, gestures, and the kinds of artifacts with which we adorn our cars or the walls of our rooms, the values and outlook of the "speaker" might be even more clear.

If one raised the academic question about naming—"What is the *best* name for X?"—the answer could not be given until another question was answered: "What do you have in mind?" Entertainer Steve Allen was once asked by a reporter whether he

45

considered himself to be essentially a comedian, a musician, a writer, or what? He replied that when he told jokes he was a comedian, when he played the piano he was a musician, when he wrote he was a writer, and when he cut the grass he was a lawn mower. Allen's deft reply is a lesson in semantics. What something "should be called" depends, in part, on the use one wishes to make of it or a particular point of view one has toward it. An item is a piece of *mail* in the mailbox, *advertising* when we read it, and *trash* when we throw it away.

Any one *thing* becomes many *things* depending on what you call it and, hence, how you look at it. Take the object you are looking at now, for example. You may classify it as a *book*, and because other objects also fit into that category, you know some of the things you can do with it. Because you regard it as *a book* you assume, without putting it to a test, that you can read it or put it on a shelf. Suppose, however, you needed to write a telephone number in a hurry and could not find a blank piece of paper. You might reclassify the book as a *source of paper* and use it for that purpose. Such a use might not have occurred to you at the time you purchased the book ("books are for reading and shelving"), but might occur later. If loose papers were blowing on the desk you might classify the book as an *object heavier than a sheet of paper* and use it as a paperweight. This object usually classified as *book* could be reclassified and used as a door prop, a decoration, a weapon, an apparatus for achieving better posture, or part of that most ambiguous classification a *well-read man*. How we classify any object or event suggests a use, a purpose. If a person thinks only in terms of one possible classification for any object, his behavior may be limited by his use of language.

There is good evidence that the most imaginative persons are those who are not bound by a single classification for an object or situation. That children are often more creative than adults may be because, lacking a comprehensive vocabulary, they are freer to treat objects as objects, not as classifications. A child may amuse himself for hours with some pots and pans because he has not bound his thinking to *cooking utensils*. Adults might be bored by that entertainment but might also feel silly—for everybody knows that pots are for cooking and not for playing.

In summary, the first dimension of language, naming, contains a utilitarian bias. When we assume that one name (and its implied purpose) is the only, best, and most appropriate name, we take our learning too seriously. Or perhaps not seriously enough. Any one *thing* may be many symbolic things, depending on our attitudes. Problems result when we fail to recognize this and associate word and thing so consistently that we think that what we usually call something is what it *really* is.[6]

The Second Dimension of Language

The child begins learning his language by discovering that everything has a name. This is what we have called the first dimension of language, the consistent association of one name with some thing. But the child may soon discover that one thing can have more than one name and that one word can stand for more than one thing. Suppose the child learns that the furry, noisy thing that licks his face is called *dog*. It is also called S*pot*. He has also heard his parents call the dog a *pet*. And he once heard his father shout, "Get that animal out of my bedroom!" And the *animal* turned out to be S*pot*. If he were an attentive child he might hear that thing called all of these names (including *that thing*) during any one day. At the point where he learns that all of these names can refer to the same thing but that some of the

---

[6]One of the greatest problems in international relations is the imposition of classifications that are meaningful in one culture onto another culture where they may not be meaningful. The ethnocentric attitude that demands that "they" see things "our way" (often disguised as the "modern," "correct," "ideal," or "practical" way) is a semantic problem of the gravest importance today. Mastering the motor skills of another language is a simple task compared to the mastery of the semantic reactions appropriate to another culture.

words include many other things as well, he is learning about the second dimension of language; in the terminology of semantics, he is learning that words are on different levels of abstraction.

Levels of Abstraction. The concept of different *levels* of abstraction is nothing new. In rather sophisticated ways, logicians and epistemologists have been aware for centuries that some words are more specific than others. Any discussion of categories, subcategories and categories of categories (even preceding Aristotle) makes this clear. What is new and what the semanticists have emphasized is that higher levels of abstraction are farther from sense data, and therefore a person who responds in the same way to a low-level abstraction (this dog Spot) as to a higher level abstraction (animal) is acting in a peculiar way. Korzybski went further. He labeled such reactions "unsane," for he reasoned that to respond to words that stand for many other *words* in the same way you react to words that stand for *things* indicates a confusion between word and thing. Such behavior is out of the realm of sense-data reality and in a world of words.[7]

To clarify the notion of levels of abstraction, look at the object that contains the page you are presently reading. Without uttering a word about it or giving it a name, observe it. Handle it. This is the sense-data that you can label *Semantics and Communication*. You may also label it a *textbook*, in which case it receives the same name as any of several other sense-data objects in your room.

---

[7]This attitude is based on an assumption that dates at least to the Thirteenth-Century conflict between the *nominalists* and the *realists*. The nominalists (including not only the present-day semanticists, but also those in the tradition of the scientific method) maintain that high-level abstractions, universals, "basic truths," and so on, do not exist except as names that are more or less useful. The realists (including the scholastics, Platonists, and many of those in the tradition of theology and metaphysics) argue that universals do indeed exist and are not "mere names." For a contemporary statement of a realist position, including an attack on the assumptions underlying this book, see Richard Weaver, *Ideas Have Consequences* (Chicago: Univ. of Chicago Press, 1947), Introduction and Chapters 1 and 8 especially.

Or you can call it a *book*, which is a little more general than *textbook*, for the word *book* includes those things that you enjoy reading. Or you can call it *printed matter*, a classification that also includes newspapers, catalogues, advertising, and postage stamps. Or you can include it among the items classified by a word like *Americana*, so that this book attains a status equal to hot dogs, frisbees, Civil War mementos, and Shaker furniture. More abstract still are words like *cultural artifact, object,* or *thing.*

Any thing can be symbolized and regarded at several different levels of abstraction. Here is an illustration by the poet e.e. cummings:

> Here is a thing.
> To one somebody, this "thing" is a totally flourishing universal joyous particular happening deep amazing miraculous indivisible being.
> To another somebody, this "same thing" means something which, if sawed in two at the base, will tell you how old it is.
> To somebody else, this "selfsame" thing doesn't exist because there isn't a thunderstorm; but if there were a thunderstorm, this "selfsame thing" would merely exist as something to be especially avoided.
> For a fourth somebody, this "very selfsame" thing, properly maltreated, represents something called "lumber;" which, improperly maltreated, represents something else called "money;" which represents something else called (more likely than not) "dear."[8]

Since we often talk about the same thing at different levels of abstraction, it is important to be aware of what we are speaking about at the appropriate level. *Chinese food* may be appropriately specific if someone asks you what kind of food you especially like. But it is hopelessly abstract in China.

If you look at any sentence at random in this book or in

---

[8]George G. Firmage, ed., *e.e. cummings: A Miscellany* (Cambridge, Ma.: Harvard Univ. Press, 1957), p. 12.

your own discourse, you will find that the various words represent several levels of abstraction. When speaking or writing, it is very difficult to maintain only one level of abstraction, be it high or low. Without such range we could not show any organization among things or indicate relationships. Also, speech that is consistently on only one level is dull and difficult to understand.

The caricature of a political speech is one bursting with highly abstract terms that may mean anything and therefore mean nothing: "Fellow Americans, let us face the future with humility, dedication, and a common purpose in the tradition of our forefathers. . . ." Democrat, Republican, radical, reactionary, and socialist could affirm these words in unison. But when they become more specific, the dissonance thunders. And, of course, social-political groups are themselves highly abstract.

There are times to be specific and times to be abstract. Our friend might put up a sign on the family gate to warn visitors: "Beware of Dog." This is sufficient; he need not post the more specific notice "Beware of Spot." On the other hand, a visitor who saw the pet and asked, "What's your pet called?" would not be helped much if the child said "a dog." Knowing what the situation calls for determines how specific or how abstract one's speech must be. It is more difficult to know whether we are *responding* to words that stand for something rather specific in the sense-data world or words that represent so many possibilities that to give one response to all of them is foolish.

Usually, the farther we go from recognizable sense-data descriptions, the more misleading our statements and responses will be.

When we consciously manipulate our symbols for some gain (as when we apply for a job and describe having worked in a service station as having been "associated with the petroleum industry" or attempt to deduct from our taxes a visit to a massage parlor as medical expense) we leap from level to level with amazing agility. We may regard these gymnastics as part of the game. But our gaming spirit is not present when we make the same leaps in the heat of prejudice or unthinking patriotism.

The idea of a vertical dimension in language (levels of abstraction) should not suggest that we can measure *specific* levels from one through twenty-five. We cannot. The idea of levels is merely a model or analogy to describe some of the differences among words. Relative to other terms we can say that a particular word is at a fairly low level, indicating rather specific conditions and qualifications of what is described. Or that a term is at a very high level of abstraction, so high that we can imagine a great many specifics that might be included in the term. But we cannot go through the dictionary and say that the first word is at the third level, the second word is at the fourteenth level, and the third word at the tenth level. Words are at our service and will be used differently by different people.

Science and Stereotypes.   High-level abstractions may be useful or worthless, the result of the most careful kind of analysis or the result of the most careless. Prejudice and stereotyped reactions toward women, Italians, and farmers can exist only on the highest levels of abstraction—the individuals within any one class are utterly different. But before we damn high-level abstractions we should note that much that is important in the social and natural sciences is also at the highest level of abstraction. Scholars who are extremely careful about their observations of the world speak of "adolescents," "middle-income groups," "enzymes," and "pressure." The difference between the biologist and the bigot is not to be found in the presence or absence of high-level abstractions in their vocabularies, but rather in the original determination of those abstractions and in the attitudes toward them.

What is important is to know how high-level abstractions were obtained, what they mean, and thus to know what cautions may be exercised in using them. I find that six tests for evaluating high-level abstractions are very useful.

1. Is the term or statement involving the high-level abstraction *tentative or final*? The laws of science are like man-made laws in that they are made to be broken. A scientific law, admittedly highly abstract, is tentative. When the law fails to account for what it claims, it is disregarded and replaced by another. When

51

the person, be he scholar or average man, speaks with unswerving faith in his generalization, he has abandoned the attitude of caution that characterizes the scientist at work.

2. Is the statement *absolute or probable*? Related to the previous test, this question reminds us that the words *never* and *always* do not appear in the vocabulary of the scientist. A statement like "children begin to talk at the age of ten months" means that *most* children do, or that your child *probably* will, and so on. It does not mean that all ten-month-olds conform to one absolute. But if words like *probably* or *tend to* or *often* were used in conversation more often, our conversations might be a little friendlier and we might be a little less demanding that the world conform to us.

3. Was the statement obtained *inductively*? In other words, how do you know what you say is true is true? Is this based on your experience? Only your experience? Or have others noted similar characteristics? The social desire to appear worldly or simply the need to make sense of the world often leads us to accept fatherly advice or common-sense statements at the higher levels of abstraction in place of careful observation at the level of experience. We must always ask how we came to know what we think we know.

4. Can the high-level abstraction be applied to a specific case? If never or rarely, the knowledge is of little value. Although this question may seem to be obvious, there is much in poetry and platitude that occupies our thinking and conversation that has almost no application. Phrases like "truth is beauty, beauty truth," or "love makes the world go 'round" are common but almost impossible to apply. When the roommate or professor speaks only of principles and is unable to give an example, we should be suspicious.

5. Can the high-level abstraction be applied to *everything*? If so, what does it tell us? In other words, does the abstraction add anything to what we already know? If not, then the comment is as useless as one that cannot be applied to anything. This test is basic to the scientific method. It is sometimes stated: given two alternative explanations or descriptions, the simpler one is

to be preferred, and all that is unnecessary should be ignored. Dating to the classical dispute between realists and nominalists and named for William of Occam, this test is known as Occam's razor (shaving away the unnecessary) or the law of parsimony. In science the word *ether* was dropped from the vocabulary when it was discovered that no ether could be detected and that none was necessary for any explanation of the passage of light, the action of gravity, or any other effect. More common examples might include the phrases that begin *theoretically*, for as often used, *everything* is theoretically possible. The words *God's will*, as they are often used mean nothing, for God's will can explain anything and therefore explains nothing.

6. Finally, does a specific abstract term exist as a useful invention or convenience, or is it regarded as a thing in itself? The term *reification* is used to describe the tendency to think that because there are certain words there must necessarily be certain things that correspond to them. To reify is to *thingify*.

Even the social scientists have been prone to reify concepts of their own invention. Words like *ego*, *id*, *collective unconscious*, and so on are reified terms when the psychologist sets about to look for *things* that correspond to those *words*. If the term is a loose way of describing certain behavior, there is no problem. But if these inventions are thought to stand for real things, confusion can be the only result.

The problems with reification are especially common when the terms are preceded by adjectives like *real* or *pure* or *true* or *essential*. There is no such thing as true love, there is only love. There is no essential man, there are only men. And so on.

Certain kinds of abstract terms, like certain expressions in abstract art, may be mixed together to produce an attractive, impressive effect. It is difficult for most of us to distinguish between abstract equations that may be inspired, concise expressions of great wisdom, and sayings that may be the result of pure whim. For example, the equation by Keats that "Beauty is truth; truth, beauty" has meaning within the context of Keats' poem *and* in and of itself. The words provoke further thought. If I pick out other high-level, abstract terms at random and substitute them for the words *beauty* and *truth*, I may also seem to go beyond mere grammatical sense. "Duty is love, love, duty" sounds like a phrase that might be uttered, even repeated, in some speech on patriotism. In the same way, I can toss together *hope, ignorance, justice, knowledge, friendship, understanding*, and many other words to produce expressions that not only make sense but occasionally seem profound.

This "mix-and-match" approach to profundity is not possible with lower level abstractions. If I proclaim that "shoe polish is popcorn, popcorn, shoe polish," people may question my sanity. But if I also choose at random very abstract terms, I may have people quoting me.

A Summary: Meaning Is as Meaning Does

Language is personal. Learned through imitating sounds that are associated with things, our language is our own, determined by the training, whims, and historical accidents of our culture, community, and family. To the extent that each person's associations and experiences are different, each person's language is a little different. Words of one speaker may sound very much like those of another. Object referents may be similar for many persons, but the experiences that determine the meaning (in response) can never be quite the same for any two people. If we recognize the arbitrary manner in which we have learned our language, we should be freer to change those semantic habits that, although they made sense to us as children, no longer seem sensible in light of additional experiences and increased understanding. Language is personal, but the *personality* of language should change as we do, and as our knowledge does.

What we call things is a matter of convention, determined by the culture in which we mature. Language requires us to divide our total experience into parts, each of which is given a name. That we need so few names to describe an infinite number of experiences demonstrates the remarkable economy of language, but at the same time it may confuse us into thinking that our experiences and perceptions are also composed of these separate elements that correspond to the language in which they are described. We must be careful not to confuse the necessity of linguistic distortion with the raw experience of the pre-symbolic world.

We have many choices of what to call things in a language. The exact words we use at a particular time reflect our attitudes and purposes at that time. What we consider important and what our society considers important will be given special attention. Often, many words will be used for what another language would recognize in only one or two words.

However, because our language habits are so pervasive, there is a *feedback* effect through which we tend to perceive those things for which we have labels and ignore those for which we do not have labels. The perceptual efficiency of seeing the verbally delineated object may also reduce the care with which we *look* at what we have labeled, with the result that we only see the label and not the thing. A person who is mature in his semantic habits will avoid being perceptually bound to his language and will attempt to see the world rather than read it.

Language, for each person, begins with naming, and for many persons, the ability to give names to things continues to be the mark of erudition. Semanticists have discouraged this overemphasis on naming things when the label becomes more important than the perception it denotes. The stage of giving names to things was called the *first dimension of language.*

From the stage of naming things, we moved to a second dimension of language, the sensitivity to different words on different levels of abstraction. Whereas some labels refer to rather specific sense data, other labels refer to abstractions of rather vague and general sense data. Our language structure offers us no clue to help us distinguish between the low-level abstractions and the higher-level abstractions, though this awareness of what we are talking about is obviously very important. If we react in similar ways to words on different levels of abstraction, our semantic behavior is confused. Sensitivity training for more discriminate reactions has been most important in the field of general semantics.

High-level abstraction, including generalizations, are extremely useful, for they help to show order and relationships. When the high-level abstractions may be clearly related to sense-data experience, these words are both convenient and important. Such high-level abstractions also characterize some language habits at their worst, for they are the basis for stereotypes and evocative terms that mean nothing because they might refer to anything. The thoughtful speaker is aware of the many things that might be designated by his words, and thus speaks with caution and qualification.

Because high-level abstractions include the most highly valued terms in our vocabulary (beauty, love, truth, justice, and so on) and because such words represent so many ambiguous but deep feelings, we may seek to objectify the terms. This behavior, reification, makes a thing of the label. With our map indicating only a word, we set out to search for a *thing*. When this happens we can only be disappointed or deluded. Put another way, instead of labeling an experience, we may attempt to experience a label.

4

Symbolic Transformation

When people are asked about the most fundamental *discoveries* or *inventions* that have shaped human society throughout history, they usually name two: the use of fire and the wheel. These seem so basic that it is difficult to imagine human beings without these earliest technologies. To these we might easily add the lever. Archimede's claim that if he had a large enough lever and a place to stand, he could move the world, reminds us of the potential of even the simplest of tools.

There is another *tool* which some might call a discovery and others might call an invention that is more fundamental and more influential than the others. This is the system of symbols we know as language. In one sense, language has given us a mobility greater than that of the wheel: by using language, we can move through time as well as space.[1]

[1]For Korzybski it was this ability to learn from the past, which he called the *timebinding* capacity, that distinguished humans from other animals. Animals survive, he said, because of their ability to move through space, fleeing danger or moving to more suitable climates or to where food is available. Humans survive

More significantly than the lever, language allows us to move the world symbolically. Our symbolic behavior, including our speaking habits, transforms a given reality into many symbolic realities. Professor Richard Dettering in his lectures on symbolism once pointed out that if you bring together a cat and a dog, the cat may cringe or run away in reaction to the dog. The way to remove the danger is to remove one of the animals. But put a child with that same dog and you have another possibility. At first the child may react to the dog in ways not so different from those of the cat, and you may still have to remove the dog (or the child). But you may also remove the threat *symbolically*: "Nice doggy," you can say reassuringly. "See, the doggy likes you."

If the symbol is such a powerful force, might it be that a particular system of symbols, with its unique vocabulary and rules, could transform the world it describes in a particular way? Might it be that because, say, Chinese and English are each different in grammar and vocabulary, that a person who grows up speaking Chinese will perceive the world in ways that are somewhat different from a person who has learned English?

Symbolic Expression as Reality

A conventional view of language is that it serves in part as a mirror which reflects an individual's thinking and actions. Of course we should expect some connection between a language and aspects of the culture in which the language is spoken: if yams are important in the culture then we should expect many words for yams, if cars are important then we should expect many words for cars. Another view of language and thought turns everything around. Rather than serving as a mirror to reflect our thoughts, language may be considered as something that actually

---

because of their ability to learn from the past and from the experiences of others as well as their own, and thus transcend the limits of their own lifetimes.

shapes our thoughts and perceptions. According to this view, language is not merely a tool for communicating what we see and think; rather, we are able to see and think only as much as our language permits. This is heady stuff. It is symbolic transformation to such an extent that we take the symbolic expression as the reality.

Such a view has been expressed for years. It was articulated by Wilhelm von Humboldt and Fritz Mauthner almost a century ago. Mauthner remarked that if Aristotle had spoken Chinese or Dakota instead of Greek, his categories would have been different. Bertrand Russell later wondered if Aristotle's philosophy might not be a projection of his language (Greek) onto his reality. Russell noted that Aristotle's *essences* looked remarkably like nouns, and his *attributes* looked curiously like adjectives.

But most of the credit for this view of the relationship between language and thought goes to two Americans, Edward Sapir and Benjamin Lee Whorf, and what has come to be known as the Sapir–Whorf Hypothesis. Sapir stated the basic idea succinctly:

> Human beings do not live in the objective world alone, nor alone in the world of social activity as ordinarily understood, but are very much at the mercy of the particular language which has become the medium of expression for their society. It is quite an illusion to imagine that one adjusts to reality essentially without the use of language and that language is merely an incidental means of solving incidental problems of communication or reflection. The fact of the matter is that the "real world" is to a large extent unconsciously built up on the language habits of the group. . . . We see and hear and otherwise experience very largely as we do because the language habits of our community predispose certain choices of interpretation.[2]

[2] Leslie Spier (ed.), *Language, Culture and Personality; Essays in Memory of Edward Sapir* (Menasha, Wis.: Sapir Memorial Publication Fund, 1941), pp. 75–93. For a collection of Whorf's work with an excellent review and interpretation, see John Carroll (ed.), *Language, Thought and Reality: Selected Writings of Benjamin Lee Whorf* (Cambridge, Ma.: MIT Press, 1956).

If you thumb through an English dictionary you will see that by far the majority of the words are nouns or words which modify nouns. The number of verbs is relatively few. In Englsh, when we use a word in a new grammatical way, the most common change is to convert a noun into, say, a verb. Words such as *research* or *format*, which used to be used only as nouns, are now commonly used as verbs as well. Our language appears to be a set of thousands of symbols, most of which represent *things*.

The Navaho language is just the opposite. Nearly all words in Navaho are either verbs or derived from verbs. Almost all nouns are passive forms of verbs or derived from verbs. Moreover, while the principal verb in English is the verb *to be*, the principal verb in Navaho is *to go*. (One imagines a Navaho Shakespeare having his Hamlet contemplate: To go or not to go/That is the question.) Linguist Gary Witherspoon writes:

> I once conservatively estimated that Navaho contained some 356,200 distinct conjugations of the verb "to go." These conjugations all apply to the ways in which humans normally "go." If we added all the verbs relating to "to move," as well as "to go" such as in walking or running, the number of conjugations would be well into the millions.[3]

Might it be that speakers of Navaho perceive a world in motion, while their Anglo neighbors perceive a much more static world of things? Anthropological descriptions of Navaho culture consistently depict a culture of movement, in art, in prayers and in other expressions.

The basic grammatical form of English (and its relatives in the Indo-European family of languages) is the subject/predicate form. Every elementary school student knows that a complete sentence must have a subject and a predicate. The subject is a kind of actor, the predicate a kind of action performed by the actor: "I am writing." "You are talking." "He is loafing." "She is

[3]Gary Witherspoon, *Language and Art in the Navajo Universe* (Ann Arbor, Mich.: University of Michigan Press, 1977), pp. 48–49.

working." We do this with nonpersonal topics too. "The sun sets." "Dew forms on the windshield." In any case, to make sense, we must have a subject and predicate—if we are to speak English correctly.

In the sentence "Tom is walking," we would say that *Tom* is the actor (the one who is doing something) and *is walking* is what Tom is doing (the action). But in the sentence "It is raining," what is the *it*? We know what *it* is doing, but what is that *it*? Ask four people who have not always lived in the desert what the *it* stands for and you may be astonished. One may say *it* means the clouds, and another will say *it* is the weather. A third will refuse to answer because he thinks there's a trick to the question, and a fourth will ask you if you are taking a course in semantics. The *it* is a fiction—as a word that represents something in reality, *it* has the same meaning as *is raining*. Our language, however, requires us to have a subject for our predicates and so we are obliged to invent one. Because grammar requires us to provide a subject for every sentence, does this also mean that we imagine that the corresponding reality is composed of subjects that do things?

While English may seem relatively static compared to Navaho, English compared to Japanese is a very *active* language—at least in its preferred forms. Teachers of journalism and English composition constantly urge students to use the active forms of verbs. Passive forms seem not only weak, they also seem to evade responsibility: the sentence "It was said that" provokes the question "Who said it?" When a political announcement from Washington appears in the passive voice, reporters may be suspicious: what is not being said, who does not want to be quoted? In Japanese, the passive voice is far more common, so that translating from Japanese to English often requires transforming passive constructions into active ones.

Mary is studious: in the present, "she studies" or "she is studying"; in the past, "she studied" or "she was studying." Predictably, in the future, "Mary will study." Our verbs divide time into three large chunks: past, present, and future. Can we describe Mary with a verb that includes all three tenses at once? Can we even think of the continuity from the past into future without dividing our thinking into the same three units determined by our verb tenses?

There are languages with very different tense systems from ours. There are languages that conjugate for ways of knowing, so that "he is here" meaning I saw him or I see him would be different from "he is here" meaning someone told me he is here or I assume so because his coat is here. Such verbs would distinguish between statements of description and statements of inference. Are English speakers more inference-prone than speakers whose language requires them to make such distinctions?

Syntactic Domain

English, like any language, has rules about what can and cannot be expressed. This is the syntactic domain. You can say "he is" or "she is" or "it is," and you can say "they are." You can also say "she are" or "they is," and you may be understood but criticized for using "improper grammar." But there is something curious about those options. In the singular, you must choose between a *he*, *she*, or *it*; setting aside *it*, you must distinguish between masculine and feminine forms. In the plural you need not, and in fact cannot, make such a distinction. These are rules of the language game, part of the system of symbols called *English*.

Obeying these rules can sometimes cause a problem. In conforming to the syntactic demands of the language, some violence may be done to the semantics. This is exactly the problem that writers have faced since the 1960s: the problem of *sexist* language. Some words could change. *Chairman* became *chairperson*; today in many places that has been shortened to *chair*, letting context make clear when one is referring to a human being— "Ms. Jameson is Chair of the Department." After a period of self-conscious changes ("Waitperson, there's a fly in my soup.") and parody ("I can't read this! Where did you learn penpersonship?"), we have settled into feeling comfortable with a somewhat de-sexed vocabulary of nouns. Still, grammar and pronouns are not so easily modified.

What would you do with the sentence "To each his own"? English allows at least three options. One is to regard *his* as a generic word meaning *hers* as well. This is the conventional view which some people are comfortable with and others are not. It is the same issue that asks whether people hearing the word *man* in expressions and book or chapter titles such as "Man the Symbol User," "The Ascent of Man," "Political Man," really imagine women in them as well. There is some evidence that when people are asked to draw what they think of when they hear such expressions, their pictures will show few, if any, women.[4]

Another option to de-sex the language is to add the phrase "or her" to expressions using "his." "To each his or her own." "Each must make up his or her mind." Some find this and other forms ("s/he") to be awkward, but it is an option within the rules of grammar.

The third option is to be ungrammatical and say "To each their own." We do this often in speech, though less often in writing. The point is that our language, even in such an apparently small instance as working with pronouns, can be very demanding.

Earlier we noted that it is not so surprising that what is important to people is likely to be reflected in their language. The example most often cited concerns the number of words for snow used by Eskimoes and others in snow countries. A Danish linguist reported more than three hundred different words used for snow in Greenland. We may assume that the distinctions reflected in the different words are significant. It is not all merely snow any more than the thousands of different items in a hardware store are all merely hardware.

We use a single word—*rice*—for that which is planted, harvested, dried, stored, cooked, and eaten. Cultures where rice is

---

[4]An excellent, if partisan, review of sexism and language is Casey Miller and Kate Swift, *Women and Words* (Garden City, N.Y.: Doubleday, 1976).

the staff of life have different words for rice in each of these stages. In Japanese the farmer plants *ine*, the shopper purchases *okome*, and people eat *gohan*.[5] It would be ludicrous to talk of "planting *gohan*" or "steaming some *ine*." Those of us accustomed to a single word have trouble understanding what difference it makes. It may be clearer in the case of the words *flour, dough,* and *bread.* We regard flour and bread as distinct; we are not likely to think of bread merely as "baked dough."

If what we know or think we know is strongly influenced by the language we speak, then even in considering this issue we may be reflecting the influence of our language. The Sapir–Whorf hypothesis may be an idea that would occur more to an English speaker than a speaker of some non-Indo-European language. So, too, would basic assumptions in general semantics be in part the product of the language in which they were first formulated and expressed.

Interdependence of Word and Thing

Anthropologist Dorothy Lee has articulated the case against the neat duality of *words* and *things* in drawing upon her knowledge of North American Indian languages.[6] Follow her reasoning as she pursues the question with reference to a hand holding a pencil:

> According to the classical view, the word is not the *thing.* This object that I hold in my hand is independent of the label I give it. It *is* not a pencil; I only assign to it the name pencil. What *it is,* is assumed to be independent of what I *call it.* Pencil is only a sound-complex, a word for the reality, the *thing.* But

[5]So important is rice to the Japanese that the equivalent words for breakfast, lunch, and supper are morning rice, noon rice, and evening rice.
[6]Dorothy Lee, "Symbolization and Value," in *Freedom and Culture* (Englewood Cliffs, N.J.: Prentice-Hall, 1959), p. 80.

64

... when I call this "pencil," I also classify it, as a substantive, a noun; I separate it as other than the fingers it elongates. Is it a *thing* before I call it a pencil?

Note that Lee is *not* asking if that object (pencil) exists of if it can be perceived or any other such question. She asks only, "Is it a *thing* before I call it a pencil?" She continues.

If it is not, then I am not "applying" a name to an already existing thing. This physical reality, this formless mass or energy, or set of relations, is delimited, is given form and substance, becomes the *thing* pencil, only through my calling it a pencil. A Maidu Indian, for example, would probably have given no recognition to, or would not have delimited this reality into, the pencil as object; instead, he would have perceived the specific act of the hand—in this case the act of pointing with a pencil—and would have expressed this by means of a suffix which, attached to the verb, "to point," means: to-point-with-a-long-thin-instrument (such as a pencil or a straight pipe, or a cigarette, or a stick). There is no reference to substance or to an object in this suffix. What is a pencil to me is a qualification or an attribute of an act for him, and belongs to a class with cigarettes and other objects of this shape only in so far as they elongate the hand making such an act possible. If this can be called a *thing*, then the symbolic process has at any rate helped create different *things* out of the physical reality.

I would say, therefore, that the classical *this* is not the *thing*, but the reality itself. At the point where it is a *thing*, it has already been made into a thing. The word and the thing are not discrete elements to be related by the speaker; they are interdependent, incapable of existence apart from and without the act of the individual.

This more sophisticated position of interdependence between word and thing seems preferable to the assumption, stated in the previous chapter, that words and things are completely separate. When we say "the word is not the thing," we have already begged the question—for what was the *thing* in the first place?

65

We would have had to *assume the existence of a discrete "thing."* Now our revised assumption is that the idea of the *thing* can come about only through symbolization. This revised position should not be confused with philosophies that deny the existence of reality entirely; nor should we think that if we have no word for *wall* we won't bump into something if we walk into what the word *wall* would symbolize. We would still be stopped by something, but *describing* that collision would be difficult. In short, *reality* is a stimulus that we shape into many *things* through symbolization (language). As soon as we talk about the *things* of the world we have already given shape to that stimulus.

Influence of Language on Thought

The idea that words and things are interdependent, that the world we know is relative to the language we speak, can be carried further. "To its logical extensions," some might say, "to extremes," critics might say.

George Orwell presented such an extreme in his powerful political novel, *Nineteen Eighty-Four*. Orwell presented a picture of a grim police state where there was almost no individual freedom. The "thought police" and the omnipresent Big Brother were always watching. The most potent force for repression, however, was not the police, but language itself. Orwell created *Newspeak*, a language "designed to diminish the range of thought" in order to prevent expression that would be contrary to the desires of the state. Orwell explains in the novel that during the early stages of the Newspeak language, it was still possible to use the word *free* in sentences such as "the field is free of weeds" or "the dog is free of fleas"; but, it was not possible to use the word *free* in order to express the human desire for freedom. Such an expression would be unsayable in Newspeak; it would be unthinkable.

Students interested in semantics are urged to read (or *re-read*, as we learn to say in college) *Nineteen Eighty-Four*. One may even find discomfiting parallels in contemporary rhetoric. The slogan "War is Peace" brings to mind the real name for one of the most destructive nuclear missiles in the American arsenal, the "Peacekeeper."

Satires illuminate through exaggeration, and so we should not forget that Newspeak is an exaggeration of the possible influence of language on thought. Linguistic relativists will prefer terms like *predispose* or *encourage* to describe possible influences of language, rather than *determines* or *controls*.

Many linguists, however, believe that even these words are too strong. They raise doubts about the significance of the observed differences in language and the possible influence on thinking. Their criticisms are many. They point to the flexibility of language to invent new terms when the need arises. The Latin that the Pope speaks includes words for things the Romans never dreamed of. Moreover, some people learn to make distinctions that their mother tongue never taught them. People who suffer from hay fever learn to make distinction among weeds that go unnoticed by those who breathe free.

Also, while those who have taken the linguistic-relativist view most seriously tend to be cultural anthropologists and others who seek to find the uniqueness of each culture, the critics tend to stress the similarities among people, and the universals of language.

There is impressive evidence that each individual is biologically equipped to generate utterances in accordance with the language spoken by those around him, but not limited to mere repetition of what he has heard. Children can construct statements that are novel even while conforming to the general rules of their mother tongue. The time and stages of first language learning appear to be the same for children all over the world, irrespective of their particular language. Both of these observations suggest to some that the most obvious differences in language are not as significant as some people might think; there is, if you will, a universality to being human that is revealed even in language. Most important in the view of this school of linguists, however, is the theory that anything said in any one language can, if it is examined at a deeper level (that is, not at the *surface* level of expression), be transformed into comparable expressions in any other language. I suspect that linguists who accept this view of language would still go along with much of the concerns of the general semanticists while denying that the root of the trouble lies in language. They would not, however, agree with the reasoning of Dorothy Lee.

Lee, of course, places far more stress on the influence of language (or symbolization)—though not to the extent that Orwell conjectured in his novel.

Unfortunately, it is no more possible to prove that "language shapes our perception of reality" than to prove the opposite, more conventional, view. Because we compare languages and translations of languages—not *perception* and certainly not *pure thought*—we are still not proving the hypothesis. And for some scholars that is sufficient reason to ignore the hypothesis. For others, this writer included, a judgment by Mark Twain applies to this subtle but important issue: "interesting, if true ... and interesting, anyway."

5

But Words Can Never Hurt Me

As children we learn to chant that sticks and stones may break our bones but words can never hurt us. Some philosophers have said very much the same thing. Ludwig Wittgenstein, for one, said that the world is independent of our will—in our terms, the world is what it is regardless of what we call it. And so it is, the semanticist agrees, with some of this world but not with all of it. The division between natural science and social science might be the distinction between worlds unaffected by language and those that are very much changed by language. The brick may not care in the least whether it is called a *brick*, or *structural material*; but the bricklayer may behave differently if he is called *laborer* or *artisan* or *construction engineer*. In the world of people, of conversation and argument, personal adjustment and insanity, words exert a tremendous influence.

In this chapter we shall apply and expand some of the principles presented earlier in order to illustrate a few of the many ways in which words influence behavior.

The Inherent Bias

No category is neutral. Not only does a classification reflect a purpose, but often an attitude is associated with the classification, too. If I were to tell you about a friend, Mr. Jackson, your attitudes toward him might vary depending on whether I said he was a college senior, a mathematics major, a football player, a poet, or a Black. It is possible that my friend can be described in all of these terms—terms *not meant* to influence a response one way or another. But your attitude might be different with each different classification. Since the meaning of any label is partly in the listener, I have no idea of what my friend Jackson might mean to you. You may like football players but dislike student poets. You may think that all mathematics majors are brilliant but most Blacks are better athletes than students. If so, clearly you are not talking about my friend Jackson, you are talking about your responses to words.

Popular persuaders—speakers, advertisers, journalists, and so on—are well aware of the impact of classification. Where a person can anticipate a generally consistent response to a term, favorable or pejorative, such a classification may be emphasized. A Chicago newspaper, for example, used to use two sets of classifications for the same state senator: one if they were commenting on actions that they approved and another if they were describing actions they did not approve. (Incidentally you should note your response to my classification of "state senator" in the previous sentence.) In one case the Senator was the "man-who-has-twice-won-the-best-legislator-award-by-the-Better-Government-Association Senator." In another context he was the "member-of-the-pro-labor-left-wing-Independent-Voters-of-Illinois Senator."

One of the popular propaganda devices is *name calling*, and students sometimes are taught that this is a nasty practice. But all labeling is *name calling*—just as the choice of the word *propaganda* is a name (a name for what *they* do—*we* present only *in-*

70

formation). The tendency is to think that labels that cause unfavorable reactions are name calling, but those that are favorable or those we habitually use are not. This is not true, of course. If we call Aaron Burr a traitor (which the court did not) and George Washington a patriot, we are calling both names.

Just as we may call what *we* disseminate *information*, and what *they* disseminate *propaganda*, we may employ an extensive *we/they* vocabulary when tensions run high or when issues are polarized. Reports during war time provide some of the most obvious examples: We gather intelligence; they have spies; we support freedom fighters; they harbor terrorists; we conduct surprise attacks; they launch sneak attacks (ambushes).

It is only when we think we have somehow totally characterized or *captured the essence* of the nonverbal world with a name that we run into difficulty. So long as we realize that no word does this and that any classification is but one of many possible, each with different attitudes and responses involved, we need not be deluded by language.

Some Words about Words about Words about . . .

Thus far we have discussed some of the ways in which words can distort our understanding of *things*, even to the point of influencing changes in those things. Another problem that results from confusing word and thing is quite different. This is the problem that is sometimes caused by the self-reflexive nature of language. That is, we may make words about things, or words about *words* about things. In the second case we are one step removed from the first case. The problem is that unless the two kinds of relations (words-for-things and words-for-words-for-things) are distinguished, we may begin to react to our own reactions.

Franklin Roosevelt's famous phrase, "We have nothing to fear but fear itself," warns of this kind of problem. It is one thing to be afraid, it is something else to be afraid of being afraid. The former may be healthy behavior, the latter a neurosis.

A common occurrence in introductory public speaking classes is the fear of speaking. It is natural for a speaker to be nervous. Few speakers ever completely lose this sensation when they first begin a speech; later, perhaps, most of the sensation of fear passes. But if a speaker is afraid of his becoming afraid, he will have much more difficulty in dealing with those tensions.

Other sensations a person feels, such as love, are natural, desirable, human. *Being in love* is one thing; *being in love with being in love* is something else. *Prejudice* is one thing; *prejudice of prejudice* is something else.

A statement that contains a reference to itself must be evaluated in a way that is different from a statement about something on the nonverbal level. This principle finds a parallel in the "theory of types," attributed to Bertrand Russell, which says that a class may not be a member of itself. Thus if I say, "There is an exception to every rule; this is a rule," I am including the statement itself in what it describes, and this creates an apparent paradox. Some of these may be amusing or entertaining puzzles to pass the time. But as the studies of interpersonal communication and psychological counseling have increasingly demonstrated in recent years, many of us employ comparable strategies for purposes that are anything but amusing. A patient tells his therapist, "Don't believe anything I tell you . . . I always lie." Is that also a lie? Or does that refer only to other subsequent utterances? Some persons (whom we might label as "sick") consciously turn their language upon itself to create confusions or paradoxes which they regard as protective. Language gives us this option.

The "That-Was-No-Lady" Syndrome

A well known framework for humor is to take one *thing* on the nonverbal level and then talk about it using two different but appropriate names that appear to be mutually exclusive. This is the basis for the classic line, "That was no lady, that was my wife," and for unintentional humor, as when one says, "He's not my friend, he's my brother." Shakespeare employed the same technique in *Henry* IV, Part I, where Falstaff swears off his thieving ways. "I must give over this life, and I will give it over," Falstaff states to his friends. When Hal immediately proposes another theft, Falstaff enthusiastically assents. Asked why the inconsistency, Falstaff answers, "Why, Hal, 'tis my vocation, Hal. 'Tis no sin for a man to labor in his vocation." In other words, "That was no sin, that was my vocation." Not all applications of the same principle result in humor.

Because any one *thing* may be classified in a variety of ways there need not be a necessary conflict between different classifications for this *same thing*. Yet we frequently make problems for ourselves when we assume that differing classifications are mutually exclusive. When we ask whether a vacation should be relaxing or energetic, we may forget that it may be both at once. When we ask whether a work of literature should tell a good story or have a message, we may forget that the best of literature may have both. When we ask whether students should take a course for knowledge or for a good grade, we may forget that the two need not conflict. These unnecessary verbal conflicts that arise in discussions I call the *that-was-no-lady-syndrome*. They frequently begin as two valuable views of the same subject and conclude as nasty arguments in which each category threatens the other one. Somewhere the humor of it all is lost.

There are areas where different labels are, within a particular system, mutually exclusive. In law, for example, it is often necessary to select one label to the exclusion of another even if to an outsider both labels seem to apply. Is X a monopoly or merely efficient production? It may be both, but in the courtroom the distinction may be necessary. Is Y perjury or merely "lapse of memory"? To a disinterested party both may apply, but the prosecution and defense will take sides. Is Z premeditated murder or an act of mercy killing motivated by love? And so on. You can probably think of many examples in politics, in ethics, in marketing, in dating customs—in any field—where the rules, stated or assumed, encourage a choice to be made among descriptions that apply equally.

When one finds a conflict that can be stated in the familiar pattern *That was no————————that was————————*, having both words apply to the same nonverbal thing, one should ask why it is necessary to argue. One does much better to return to the nonverbal world for closer scrutiny than to haggle over two words.

This suggestion may seem to be a superficial and naive approach to the solution of many of life's conflicts, and for some problems I am sure it is. If, however, you will take the trouble to apply the test of non-mutual-exclusion, I think that you will find that often it is useful. You may find, too, that the unnecessary verbal conflict is the more naive attitude.

The Narrowed Vision

The previous discussion has dealt with terms that need not be mutually exclusive but which are treated as if they were. A still more common problem is the tendency to select mutually exclusive categories that are unnecessary in the first place. As soon as we select categories that are limited and extreme (at opposite poles) we are asking for trouble.

When our categories become narrowed, our perceptual world may become narrowed, too. This is most common and possibly most dangerous when we divide the world into only two categories—good or bad, right and wrong, black or white. Semanticists use the term *two-valued orientation* for this tendency, at term roughly equivalent to the *disjunctive fallacy* of classical logic. Korzybski believed that the two-valued orientation was encouraged by the second law of Aristotelian logic (the law of the excluded middle), which says that everything is either A or *not*-A. In some systems,

74

the logic is valid and appropriate.[1] In everyday application, how-ever, the dichotomy is not so practical.

Korzybski was highly critical of what he called the two-valued orientation and proposed instead that we maintain a multivalued orientation. A simple analogy may illustrate the difference. Com-pare the on/off switch of a radio or hi-fi set with the knob that controls the volume. With the former there are only two possi-bilities: either the set is on or it is off. But once it is on, the volume may be turned so low as to seem to be off, or it may be turned full blast. If there are a few people in the room, we might note, all will readily agree that the set is on or off. But they may disagree completely about just where to set the volume. This analogy may help to explain one reason the two-valued orien-tation is attractive in some cases for some persons: it makes choices and agreement apparently simpler. Unfortunately—or fortunately—the world seems more accurately and more richly described in terms of degrees and gradations.

Are there any events that have only two clear-cut possibil-ities? Life and death used to seem like the most obvious ex-amples, even though Eastern philosophers have traditionally ar-gued that these were not at all opposites but rather part of the same reality. In many cases, of course, there is no disputing that one person is alive and that one is dead. But there are some cases where the change is not so clear, and far from being a semantic problem, the issue can involve interpretations from bi-ology, medicine, law, and ethics. Only a few years ago there was common agreement that a person was dead when the person's heart stopped beating. Now, of course, it is possible to revive once-stilled hearts or even to transplant hearts. Thus the brain has come to be the critical organ in determining death for many doctors and according to some laws. At this point, however, it

---

[1]Some critics have argued that even for Aristotle's day, the two-valued logic was unnecessarily limiting. See Hans Reichenbach, *The Rise of Scientific Philosophy* (Berkeley: University of California Press, 1959), pp. 215–218.

is possible for a person to be alive, according to some criteria, and dead according to others.

Are there other events which are appropriately symbolized as either/or, two-valued alternatives? Are there other events which cannot accurately be described as more or less, to some degree, a little bit, or mostly? Can the girl be a little bit pregnant? There are situations in which one makes a choice to do something or not to do something—to find the plaintiff guilty or not guilty (though this is clearly the application of a label to a very complex nonverbal event), to marry or not to marry (and, of course, here there are marvelous compromises, too).

During times of stress, the number of apparent choices narrows. A common technique of persuasion is to play upon tensions by polarizing alternatives, one of which is appealing, the other hardly a viable choice. Will you be saved or will you be damned? Are you part of the solution or are you part of the problem? America: love it or leave it.

Certain mental abberations have been described in terms of the two-valued orientation—the paranoiac who evaluates his world in terms of threats or nonthreats, for example. In his fine book, *People in Quandaries*, Wendell Johnson presents the argument that many mental disturbances can be traced to semantic disorientations.[2] Johnson believes that many serious problems are reflected in the two-valued orientation. Healthy people, he argues, are more comfortable with many classifications for acts and other people, whereas the disturbed person is happiest when he has only to choose between two possibilities.

Some of Johnson's conclusions have been challenged.[3] The authors of *The Measurement of Meaning* state that "If anything, results suggest that normals are more comfortable in the neat dichotomies than are neurotics." Because different approaches were used in the studies, there is no need to support one view or the

---

[2] Wendell Johnson, *People in Quandaries* (New York: Harper and Row, 1946), pp. 294–335.
[3] Charles E. Osgood, George J. Suci, Percy H. Tannenbaum, *The Measurement of Meaning* (Urbana, Ill.: University of Illinois Press, 1957), p. 250.

other. There are neurotic tendencies to be squeamish about making any decision, and there are defensive tendencies in which outsiders are classified as threatening or non-threatening. Moreover, the distinction between *normal* and *disturbed* persons is deceptively two-valued.

It is sufficient to recognize that any verbal system is arbitrary and that no matter how many ways we slice up the world we are still distorting it. But to limit the number to just two possibilities is extremely distorting and is a semantic problem to be avoided if at all possible.

Caught in the Act

It is a characteristic of the English language that although our verbs have specific tenses, our nouns rarely offer temporal clues. Thus, we can use different tenses of the verb *to go* and say "the boy goes," or "the boy will go," or "the boy went," but we cannot easily construct a sentence that would include all of those possibilities. However, with a noun, like *boy*, the opposite is true. There is nothing in a noun (or adjective) that indicates its position in time and space. Although there is an obvious convenience to such indefinite, all-time nouns, they may also present us with many problems if we are not careful.

If I write about Roman Catholics or Republicans or fraternities, I apparently must include all that has been classified under these labels. I may, if I choose, add additional words of qualification—"the Roman Catholics in Spain, 1503" or "the Roman Catholics at the Second Ecumenical Council"—which make the term a little more specific. A sampling of daily conversation would probably indicate that we prefer to speak of mass nouns and adjectives rather than take the trouble to be more specific.

Korzybski suggested adding subscripts to our general terms to make them more precise. Thus we would speak not of Chicago politics but of Chicago politics$_{1965}$ and Chicago politics$_{1985}$ and so on. Rather than extoll or condemn "the free enterprise system," we would do better to speak of "the free enterprise system _{railroads, 1880s}" or "the free enterprise system _{Willy's Rib Shack, 1980s}." Although such notations may not do much for one's prose style, they might do a great deal for clarity of expression. Between style and precision, Korzybski's preference was clear.

Instead of thinking of yourself as *me*, it is wiser to indicate different *me's* for different years and in different situations. This might call attention to the obvious fact of change and growth that is significant but often obscured under the label *me*. It is popularly believed that each person has something of an *essence* or *core* that never changes and is the *basic person* or the *authentic person*. I am not sure that this is a very realistic view for a lifetime, though our language habits certainly encourage the attitude. It can be argued that an individual at any particular time shares more characteristics with others of the same age and background than the person does with himself or herself from the cradle to the grave. Indeed it is this commonality that permits scientific studies in human behavior. The point here is not that we change our names periodically to mark our growth and behavioral change, but merely that we remember that there is much change that can be concealed by using the same name over a relatively long period of time.

Very closely related to this tendency to conceptualize *things* indefinitely is the habit of verbally extending a single event into a pervasive characteristic. There is a difference between saying "Arthur lied to me last Tuesday," and saying "Arthur is a liar." Many persons utter sentences of the second kind when the more accurate statement would be the first one. Or take this pair of sentences: "Louie murdered his aunt last September" and "Louie is a murderer." Here the confusion between the two is still more common, as a glance at the morning paper might show. Some people might reason, "Of course we all lie now and then but that doesn't make us *liars*; but once you murder somebody you definitely *are* a murderder." And yet the principle of extending a single event to a total description is the same in both cases. It is just that we have stronger feelings about murder than we do about lying.

Using generalized labels saves time and effort. In the process, of course, our thinking and communication is clearly distorted. What is worse, such labels often stick and even become the basis for other inferences that compound the distortion. We may avoid the subtle dangers of generalized labels if we take the trouble to be more specific and state the conditions under which the label is applied.

Living up to the Label

Sometimes words are instrumental in actually changing what they describe. Labels which may have been given to characterize one person's impression of another at some particular place and time may stick. In such a case the words may seem to express something of the nature of the person, and so predict that person's behavior.

We always have the potential of becoming what the label implies. We can live up to our labels whether they have been applied by others ("the shy one," "just a dumb jock," "your typical class clown") or by ourselves.

Wendell Johnson wrote extensively on the problem of stuttering, believing that persons become stutterers only after they have been called "stutterer." By being given a name that calls attention to an otherwise temporary speech difficulty ("I think our Johnny is a stutterer"), the child becomes curious, begins to respond to the new label, and in his responses he "becomes a stutterer." Without a word to give significance to his behavior, it is possible Johnny would not have continued to have such problems.

Often there is comfort in responding to a label. You may prefer to say "I am a Libra" or "I am a chess freak" than to have no such label at all. If you label yourself as "no good in math" or "a lousy public speaker" or "the quiet type," you may continue to prove that this is so. Responding to such labels gives us direction, even if the direction is backwards; responding to such labels helps us decide what to do and what not to do, even if the choices are not the wisest. In such behavior we fail to recall the circumstances under which the label was first applied and the degree to which our interpretation of the situation determined our choice of label.[4]

Saying it May Make it So

It is clear that a person's attitude, self-esteem, and behavior can be affected by the label the person has come to accept. It is also possible that large numbers of other people, entire institutions, even events in history can be altered in part by what is said about them.

In 1982, a syndicated stock market analyst predicted that the stock market would drop significantly, and so recommended to his large number of readers that they sell quickly. Two things happened. His readers and many others who heard his prediction did sell; and, as predicted, the prices of stocks plunged. One interpretation is that the adviser had the foresight to see what was going to happen, and he had the facilities to warn his followers. Another interpretation is that because so many people thought the market would drop, they quickly sold, which itself caused the market to drop. This latter interpretation is an example of what has come to be known as the "self-fulfilling prophecy," a phenomenon first identified by sociologist Robert K. Merton.

[4]For a vital theory of personality related to the tendency to live up to labels, see Carl Rogers, *Client-Centered Therapy* (Boston: Houghton Mifflin, 1951), pp. 481–533.

Note that the self-fulfilling prophecy works only when the area about which the prediction is made may, in some way, be acted upon by the person making the prediction. It does not apply to statements like "It will not rain tomorrow.

The potential of the self-fulfilling prophecy is extraordinary. Suppose, for example, you label students on your campus or neighbors in an apartment building you have just moved into *unfriendly*. Your label is itself a kind of prediction: it suggests what kind of behavior you may and may not expect from the others. How, then, should you act, if what you predict is accurate? You certainly should not bother going out of your way to be friendly yourself. And if others perceive your behavior accordingly you will find that sure enough, the people just aren't friendly.

In some stunning research conducted in the 1970s, it was found that teachers can easily get the kind of performance from students that they expect. Students were randomly divided into groups which were then arbitrarily identified as either exceptionally good students or as mediocre or poor students. In fact, there was no demonstrable difference, and of course nothing was said about this to the students themselves. The research showed clearly that when teachers thought their students were bright and eager, the students tended to act that way. When teachers were led to believe that their students were of lesser ability, the students tended to perform that way. The reasons lay not in the students, but rather in the students' responses to the teachers who unwittingly communicated different expectations based on what they had been told.

Reasons for a person's failing at any number of things—failing an examination, losing a game, giving up trying to do something—are likely to include some influence of the self-fulfilling prophecy. If you have a test in the morning and you predict you cannot pass, then it is only smart not to bother studying. And not studying is very likely to help your prediction to come true. If a team knows it can't win, it is less likely to try and thus very likely to cause the prediction to come true.

If country A predicts that country B is hostile, it is likely that country A will strengthen its defenses against country B. But if country B sees A strengthening its defenses while making ominous statements about the bellicose nature of country B, what should we expect B to do? And so B also strengthens its defenses against A which, of course, confirms A's prediction. This in turn calls for further defense build-up, followed by a reciprocal build-up of the B forces, and so it goes.

This pattern is known by several names—the arms race, the arms spiral, escalation, and so on—and it is the most frightening of self-fulfilling prophecies.

Symbolic Strategies

It was the literary and rhetorical critic Kenneth Burke who gave the name *symbolic strategies* to the ways in which we may manipulate our symbols in lieu of altering reality. In one sense all of language and thought is a strategy for coming to symbolic terms with that muddled world of process and change. Every time we impose order on the outside world through language, we are applying some kind of strategy. Apart from the overall function of language, there are some special strategies, peculiar and often personal, by which we come to grips with things. We will consider four of these.

Possess the Symbol.   One form of symbolic strategy is the apprehension of symbols when what the symbols represent is difficult or nearly impossible to obtain. Our mass society today can supply the symbols of almost everything to almost anybody with a few dollars to spend. Symbols of power, love, status, sex, and even humility may be represented in cars, pins, homes, magazines, or clothing.

Every year thousands of books on such varied subjects as winning friends, effective speaking, writing for profit, improving your memory, and learning hypnotism, are sold to persons who will never try to develop these skills. It is enough for these people to study the symbols of the skills. For most of us, having that knowledge, which means *owning* some great books, knowing some special words, or taking *that* course, is our way of dealing with what those symbols represent.

Fool Thyself.   We probably all know people who make it a habit to set their clocks and watches five or ten minutes ahead of standardized time. Such persons usually claim that this manip-ulation always gives them the extra few minutes they need when their clocks show them to be a little bit late. The logic of this self-deception is not altogether clear to me, but apparently it works for some people. It is another kind of symbolic strategy. Or take the example of students who have taken examinations but who have not yet received their grades. It is not uncommon for the students to tell themselves that they did more poorly than they think they did. By fooling themselves in this way, the students believe they cannot be disappointed when the grades are announced.

   Such symbolic strategies are not necessarily harmful because the deceptions are intentional and directed only to the individual. There may be elements of superstition or even ritual involved in such habits, too, but the underlying principle is to manipulate symbols in order to fool oneself in some vaguely useful or pro-tective way.

Identification.   Another variety of these symbolic strategies is the temporary identification with other persons who seem to have things under control. When we enjoy a Western movie because it depicts a world in which the lines are clearly drawn between good and bad, right and wrong we are entering symbolically a world that is more manageable than our own. We need only identify with the man-in-control to feel more important and more responsible. Such identification frequently lasts for some time after the program, film, book, or other vicarious experience, has ended. It is probably no accident that Westerns became adult fare on television during a time when the "real world" of the news reports was becoming increasingly confused. To find a world that we can deal with, we may escape to fantasies, biographies of famous people, or various melodramas. Much of the popular evocative rhetoric, in political speeches, sermons, commencement-day addresses, and the like, may serve the same function.

Mittyism. Instead of turning to the symbols produced for our identification by professionals, we may create our own fantasies. We have the choice of becoming a giant in a world of midgets, or of remaining ourselves and cutting the world down to our size. James Thurber's Walter Mitty is a famous example of the former approach, though what Thurber depicted is by no means limited to fiction. Much of our sleeping activity, dreaming, appears to be normal and necessary to symbolically reestablish our position in the world. Such unconscious symbolic activity begins at a very early age. There is speculation, for example, that some young children who wet their beds are symbolically trying to drown their parents, an act that out-Mittys Mitty. In more familiar and conscious form is the employee who, among his co-workers, pokes fun at his boss because he cannot physically poke his boss. Other similar symbolic strategies go under the names of ridicule, sarcasm, and many kinds of jokes.

In order to give importance to ourselves and our problems we may prefer to remain as we are but involve the whole world with our problems. On the day of a difficult final examination, for example, you may think, "Maybe the college will burn down so I won't have to take it." Although this approach may seem more perverse and more cowardly, it may be no less common. Either way—to inflate yourself to be bigger than the big awful world, or to bring the world down to your size—the principle of manipulating symbols to deal with reality is in effect.

When we manipulate our symbols in order to deal with the world in a way that is comforting to us we are not necessarily acting in an unhealthy manner. For catharsis, for a boost in morale, or for a first step toward action, such strategies may be as healthy as they are common. But if we feel that we have altered something in the nonverbal world when we have only played with symbols, or if we escape to symbols so often that we cannot face up to the real problems, or if we confuse our imaginative world with what passes for the real world, then we may find ourselves in serious trouble.

Sticks and stones may break our bones but words can never hurt us. Would that it were true. Injuries from sticks and stones can be repaired—or, if not, then at least we can collect on the insurance. The harm that words can cause is more subtle and sometimes more permanent. And, except in rare cases, there is no insurance policy that can even acknowledge the semantic damage. Moreover, it is the odd person who abuses himself with sticks or stones, but rare is the individual who does not suffer from some self-afflicted semantic wounds.

In this chapter we have reviewed some of the problems we create through language, and issued some general warnings and suggestions. Let the thinker beware. But let him not therefore stop thinking and speaking.

6

"Nice" Words and "Bad" Words

There are certain subjects and certain words about which people take special care, subjects that we don't talk about in *polite* company or words we don't use in *mixed* company (though that term may be disappearing). There are words that the Federal Communications Commission will not allow to be said on the radio or on television, or which when used in a movie require the producers to forewarn potential viewers. The use of some of these words will provoke parents to wash out their child's mouth with soap. What a lesson in semantics that teaches! And millions of adults, who believe they are somewhat sophisticated about the word–thing relationship and the nature of symbols, will still be affected by some of these words. We may blush or cringe or stare at the floor. These are what some call *bad* words or *dirty* words or what we shall call *tabooed* words.

There are other words which are *polite* and which are intended to avoid any unpleasant provocation. These are *nice* words, or what we will call *euphemisms*. The subject of taboo and euphemism is of more than passing interest. It may help us to understand better some of the complexity of the word–thing relationship, and may in the process help us test some of our deeply rooted semantic attitudes and values.

What is improper to speak of or to symbolize in one culture may be quite innocent in another. Many people in the United States and some Western societies are made nervous by the number thirteen. (Fear of the number thirteen even has its own name: *triskadaikophobia*.) Even modern hotels often omit that number for identifying a floor; elevators skip from twelve to fourteen. Why is it we are bold enough to send a man to the moon but not to the thirteenth floor of a Hilton Hotel? Explanations for superstitions often are based in folk theories: one explanation for our attitude towards the number thirteen dates back to the thirteen men present at Christ's last supper.

In Japan the numbers four and nine are to be used with care. In this case the fears are *homophonic*, or based on similar sounds. The sound for four is *shi*, which is also part of the sound of the word for death; *ku*, the sound for nine, can also mean suffering.

In Moslem countries there is a very clear distinction between what is done with the right hand (the clean hand) and what is done with the left hand (used for certain unclean acts). The sole of the foot or shoe likewise is associated with what is unclean. Thus, using the left hand improperly or baring the sole of the foot can be taken as grave insults. On the other hand, so to speak, gesturing with one's middle finger pointed straight up, an obscene act in the United States, will go unnoticed.

While this country still retains some sense of modesty toward exposure of women's breasts, the exposure of legs is today more a matter of fashion than decency. In many parts of the world, the reverse has been true.

Taboo or Not Taboo

It is strange and strangely understandable that the subjects for which we are most careful about choosing our words are basic to the human condition: sex, the very basis of existence; death, the termination of earthly existence; and certain parts of the body and the exudations, secretions, and other involuntary actions associated with those parts. Each of these subjects is laden with symbolic significance, but also each is more a *necessity* of life than, say, clothing or shelter. Even though many of these words refer to what may be called *facts of life*, they are regarded much more emotionally than other *facts about life*. People do not become squeamish about breathing. Eating is somewhere in between as there are tabooed foods and manners and sometimes care in choice of words (in an elegant setting, with tablecloth and candles, one would probably *dine* rather than *eat*).

One intriguing theory of what is tabooed has been put forth by the English anthropologist Edmund Leach[1]. It might be regarded as a semantic theory, since it is based on feelings about categories and a version of *either/or* logic. Leach begins with an assumption that the child perceives the social and physical world as a continuum. Only by learning a language is that world divided into distinct categories. It becomes important for the child to distinguish between what is part of the child and what is not, for example. (Psychologists have made much of what may be an extremely influential experience of learning: that mother is not an extension of the child.) There remain, however many gaps between discrete *things* distinguished by language and things left undistinguished, things that seem to be both of one sort and another at the same time. There are things each child must feel are both *me* and *not me* at the same time. In Leach's view, these are likely to become tabooed—either regarded with fear or embarrassment, or, in some cases, venerated.

Fish are water creatures, animals are land creatures, but reptiles are both, and in cultures everywhere these are likely to be feared, killed by people, and for the most part considered inedible. In the human world, that which is somehow both *me* and *not me* is likely to be tabooed, perhaps because it is mysterious and

---

[1]Edmund Leach, "Verbal Categories and Animal Abuse," in Eric Lenneberg (ed.), *New Directions in the Study of Language* (Cambridge, MA.: MIT Press, 1967).

frightening. For the child, *bodily wastes*, to use a euphemism, are one of the first things he learns about which fits this criterion. Similarly the sexual act and conception are ambiguous. And so, too, with death—when we seem to be both of this world and yet not.

This theory extends to how we classify what can be eaten and what cannot. Pets, for example, are in that ambiguous zone between *non-human* and *one of us*. Leach also believes that animals invoked for the purpose of verbally abusing or cursing others are those which are closest and most familiar to us; unfamiliar animals, no matter how fearsome, are not used to curse others. Think of your favorite invective that refers to animals and you will probably see that this fits. When was the last time you heard someone called a "son of buffalo?"

What seems consistent is that whenever there is something that embarrasses or frightens us, we will be careful about how we talk about it. We may find alternative, nicer sounding words—euphemisms. We talk around it, using circumlocutions. ("You know who is doing you know what!") We may avoid any mention of it—or try to.

This means that we can usually tell what it is that embarrasses or frightens us by listening to how we talk. Let's consider three tabooed areas and associated words more carefully, for each has its own peculiar features.

Death

No word associated with death that comes to mind is likely to be penciled out by an editor or publisher or even objected to by readers. I can write *death* or *dead* or *die* or *bury* or *cremate* or even *corpse* and probably no one will be shocked, no one will blush. Even as invective, telling someone to *drop dead* will probably not be as upsetting as refering to the same person by some slang term for a part of the anatomy. Nevertheless, if one wishes to send a sympathy card to someone who has had a death in the family, no card will include any of these words for death. At the funeral mourners may be careful not let slip the words *die* or *dead* or *death*.

The reason is, in part, cultural. Mexican poet and essayist Octavio Paz has written eloquently of such differences when it comes to talking of death:

> The word death is not pronounced in New York, in Paris, in London, because it burns the lips. The Mexican, in contrast is familiar with death, jokes about it, caresses it, sleeps with it, celebrates it; it is one of his favorite toys and his most steadfast love.[2]

Though the cultures of the United States and Mexico remain very different in this regard (compare Halloween with Mexico's Day of the Dead celebrations, for example), there have been changes in this country concerning death in recent years. People are now encouraged to talk about death more openly, and there are many seminars, books, and articles on dying and death. Nevertheless, our stock of euphemisms related to death remains one of our largest and most used. Think of all the words about death you are familiar with; including slang, the average person has no trouble in thinking of fifteen or more words.

Many of the euphemisms are religiously inspired: *gone to her reward, gone to meet his maker, gone to a better life.* Many are more vague about the destination: *passed away, gone away, left us, departed.* Then there are euphemisms that emphasize the feelings of the living, such as speaking of one's *loss.*

It seems clear that the intent in these cases is to spare the feelings of others who are pained by the death of a loved one. We do not ordinarily use euphemisms when speaking of people who were not personally known to us or to those with whom we are speaking, nor do we use euphemisms about people who have

---

[2]Octavio Paz, *The Labyrinth of Solitude* (New York: Grove Press, 1957), p. 3.

died long ago. We do not say that "George Washington passed away in 1799."

When there are many deaths at a particular time and there is heightened awareness that people we know might die, we are likely to find more euphemisms. On certain holiday weekends, for example, the National Safety Council announces reports of deaths in automobile accidents. These are likely to be euphemized as *fatalities*. ("Don't become a statistic!" was one grim warning.) During wartime (odd how a term like *wartime* seems almost like a season), euphemisms will be used to keep up morale. During World War I, new troops sent to Europe were for a time called *replacements*; this was later changed to *reinforcements*. Reporting deaths on "our" side is likely to be more vague (*heavy losses*) than reports of deaths on the other side. This kind of practice reached its height during the Viet Nam war when the *body count* of the enemy was announced with the regularity of a stock market report.

There are slang euphemisms such as *kick the bucket* or *pushing up daisies*. With slang, old expressions generally fall out of use while others enter the vocabulary: *checking out* is one of the more current terms.

Professions that confront death constantly have their own euphemisms, some of which enter popular usage. Hospitals have an extensive euphemistic vocabulary for dying or dead patients. DNR may be written on the hospital chart of a terminal patient near death; to a casual visitor it might go unnoticed, but to the staff it stands for *Do Not Resusitate*. Hospital attendants may use slang expressions which are euphemistic and intended to help them cope with and manage constant emotional strain. Terminal cases may be *short-term visits*, and a person with serious multiple injuries may be a *crunch case*.

A personal favorite euphemism for a hospital patient who has died is *negative patient care outcome*. Taking this along with a Reagan Administration euphemism for taxes, *income enhancement*, one reporter suggested a modern version of a famous Ben Franklin adage: Nothing is certain in this life but negative patient care outcome and income enhancement.

91

The funeral profession, of course, has the most extensive euphemistic vocabulary of all and has actively sought to introduce its terms to the general public. If you look in the yellow pages for *undertakers* you are likely to be directed to *funeral directors*. Graves become *final resting places*, caskets become *slumber boxes*. The *cemetery*, once a euphemism for *graveyard*, is now more likely to be called a *memorial garden* or *park*. All of this is for the benefit of the dead, more correctly called in the land of foreverness, *the loved ones*.

The Body and the Process of Elimination

Probably the first words children are taught not to say, as well as the first for which they are taught euphemisms, concern elimination. That is, words concerning urinating and defecating. Those particular words, however, are rarely used by parents, as they seem technical or clinical. This is true of the semantics of taboos in our society: we have two sets of words, one that seems too technical for casual use, and the other that seems too vulgar for polite use. Euphemisms, including slang and baby-talk, are often the only words that occupy some middle area.

In a single kindergarten class, teachers may hear a repertoire of two or three dozen euphemisms children have learned to use when they *have to go to the bathroom*, *have to go*, *have to*, and so on. Adults know even more.

Bathroom itself often has nothing to do with a bath but is simply a euphemism of the word *toilet*. *Toilet* irritates some people, but it was once a euphemism, too. It is the usual fate of euphemisms to become eventually as unpleasant as the words they initially replaced. Such was the case of *cemetery*, which replaced *graveyard*. Probably any American over fifteen knows a dozen or more words or phrases like *the john*, *the head*, *the ladies room*, *the gents*, *the* W.C. Many of these, including *the john*, have a history that can be traced back for centuries.

Tabooed words, however, are likely to be far older than any

of the words that might have served as euphemisms. The word *shit*, for example, has been around for more than four hundred years. Many of these words are rightly called *Anglo-Saxon* words. At the time of the Norman conquest, the ruling class spoke French, but the peasants spoke English. Today many of our euphemisms derive either from French or Latin, while the "coarse language" remains Anglo-Saxon.

Sex

Sex is a three letter word, but some would argue that *sex* as it is often used is itself more of a euphemism than a tabooed word. If a society can be known by its words, what it talks about most, and how it talks, then surely this society places a far higher value on sex than almost anything else. This is all the more remarkable for how different things are from not so many years ago, when sex was notable for how much it was not talked about.

People speak of the "sexual revolution" with a confidence that obscures the very complicated and numerous changes that have taken place in the United States and abroad during the past quarter century. Some changes were technological, such as development of *the pill* and other contraceptive technologies. Others were social and economic changes, including an increase of women in the work force. Families where mothers remain at home with the children amount to only fourteen percent. Legal changes followed, allowing more explicit images and "obscene" words to be printed, or expressed on film, records, television, or other media. It seems surprising to young people today that only a few years ago, a film maker had to fight in court to allow the word *pregnant* to be said in a movie; it seems incredible that only a generation before that, the Hollywood motion picture code requested that no udders be shown on the cows that appeared in Mickey Mouse cartoons.

Aldous Huxley's prophetic novel *Brave New World* describes

a future society where reproduction entails test-tube babies being *decanted* in a sterile baby factory.[3] In one scene, a group of school children are being given a tour of the factory by the director. In telling the young visitors about some event in history, the director uses the word *parents*. He stops and asks the children if they know what *parent* means.

> There was an uneasy silence. Several of the boys blushed. They had not yet learned to draw the significant but often very fine distinction between smut and pure science. One, at last had the courage to raise a hand.
> "Human beings used to be ..." he hesitated; the blood rushed to his cheeks. "Well, they used to be viviparous."
> "Quite right." The Director nodded approvingly.
> "And when the babies were decanted ..."
> " 'Born,' " came the correction.
> "Well, then, they were the parents—I mean, not the babies, of course; the other ones." The poor boy was overwhelmed with confusion.
> "In brief," the Director summed up, "the parents were the father and the mother." The smut that was really science fell with a crash into the boys' eye-avoiding silence. "Mother," he repeated, rubbing in the science ...

The novel is satire, but the point that what was once considered quite natural and human can become tabooed, occurs more often in the real world than in science fiction novels. Many people today still speak of the meat of chicken or turkey as *light meat* and *dark meat*. These terms were euphemisms which became popular during the Victorian era in order to avoid saying *breast* and *legs*. Those words were too suggestive, too much like smut, in Huxley's terms, even when applied to an animal.

During the Victorian era, one would avoid many words that today seem so *normal* that it is difficult to think of alternative expressions, let alone feel the need for any. Even the names of articles of clothing were affected. Women's *underwear* had a eu-

[3]Aldous Huxley, *Brave New World* (New York: Harper & Row, 1939), p. 44.

phemism in French, *lingerie*, and the no-nonsense euphemism, *unmentionables*. Animal terms, if at all associated with sexuality, were altered: *donkey* replaced *ass*, for awhile *he-cow* replaced *bull*, and *bitch* became *lady dog*. Many people today still feel uncomfortable with the older terms, an indication of how easy it is to confuse *smut* and *science*.

As with other euphemisms, those related to sex may last for a long time as euphemisms or may acquire some of the unsavory connotations of the words they were to replace. *Sexual intercourse*, for example, was just such a euphemism a century ago, replacing *copulation*. The word *intercourse* had been associated with any kind of social interaction, including conversation, and occasionally is still used that way: "I'm sorry to be late, class, but I was having intercourse on the library steps." For most Americans today, however, the most immediate if not exclusive meaning of intercourse is sexual. As a result, the word has lost much of its euphemistic effectiveness. Other expressions, however, seem to last forever. According to a recent thesaurus of euphemisms, the expression *to sleep with* someone is more than a thousand years old.

There is something special about the semantics of some tabooed subjects, with their vulgar and euphemistic words and phrases. The tabooed words often serve more different functions of communication than do most *ordinary* words. (See Chapter 8.) Both in theories of why there are tabooed subjects as well as in the intensity of the reactions of some people, there is an indication of *word magic*—as if saying or even thinking a certain word will cause something terrible to happen. When used as expletives, the words provide catharsis: they help to release feelings of anger or stress or pain. The general principle is that the greater the hurt, the stronger the language. In intimate situations between lovers, some terms become the most intense expressions of erotic love, and thus their meaning is primarily affective. And, of course, they may be primarily terms of description or reporting, though it is in that function that some critics will ask, "Why do you have to use that word?" as if the words were interchangeable. (This calls to mind a story that used to be told about President Harry

Truman who was noted for his earthy language. A friend of Mrs. Truman suggested she persuade the President to use the word *fertilizer* instead of *manure* in his speeches. The First Lady replied, "My goodness, it's taken me twenty years to get him to say *manure*.")

The issue of taboo and euphemism is complex. Some people argue that if people had a more scientific, realistic understanding of the body, sexual relations, human mortality, and other subjects which can become tabooed, then these elaborate systems of words to avoid words to avoid discussing what is natural would just disappear. They contend that even with the greatly increased freedoms of what can be printed or expressed in films, there is still an attitude toward some words that might be regarded as fetishism, where the sound or shape of a word will arouse passions. Other people argue that we need such signal reactions for catharsis (see Chapter 9). They reason that it is normal and healthy for these "special words" to refer to what is still for most people highly personal and mysterious.

How a person feels about this subject certainly depends on his or her current values, but it also depends on the attitudes fostered in childhood. Likewise, we should expect that a person's view toward taboo and euphemism will be reflected in what that person will try to encourage in his or her children. It is curious how we sometimes say we believe one thing but prefer to teach our children something slightly different. You might ask yourself, what would you teach your child?

The past few decades have seen a general liberalization toward some previously tabooed words, particularly those concerning death and sex. Are there other topics which, to judge from the ways we talk or avoid talking about them, are subjects which embarrass and frighten us? Surely there are many, but here are two to consider briefly.

Tom uses a wheel chair. Dick is blind. Harry looks *normal* but he cannot hear; he reads lips to understand others, and he speaks in a manner that is noticeably different from Tom and Dick. Many people who talk with Tom, Dick, and Harry avert their eyes, lest they seem to be staring.

Many people are unsure of how to refer to each of these people or to all of them collectively. They may not even be sure which words are *bad* and which are *nice*, or at least socially acceptable. When talking with Dick they embarrass themselves when they inadvertently say something like, "Do you see what I mean?" Yet if they listened to Dick speak they would hear him say the same thing; he knows the difference between the meanings of the two usages of "see."

People who are blind are likely to be aware of the efforts that sighted people sometimes make to avoid using the word *blind*. Harold Krents, a lawyer who is blind, tells of what he encounters and his reactions:[4]

> When I go to the airport and ask the ticket agent for assistance to the plane, he or she will invariably pick up the phone, call a ground hostess and whisper . . . "We've got a 76 here." I have concluded that the word *blind* is not used for one of two reasons: either they fear that if the dread word is spoken, the ticket agent's retina will immediately detach, or they are reluctant to inform me of a condition of which I may not have been previously aware.

The 1980s began with the United Nations International Year of the Disabled Person. Attention was drawn to millions of people all over the world who are often ignored or disadvantaged more by social attitudes and policies than by their own physical limitations. Most of these are reflected in semantic habits, which in turn reflect fear, embarrassment, and ignorance in society. The greatest handicap is a semantic one.

We also find an embarrassment in words related to aging. By the year 2020, the number of Americans over the age of 65 is expected to be twice what it is today. This society, which has from its beginning valued the qualities of youth, will be populated with a very large number of people who are *old*. But right now,

[4]Barbara Baskin and Karen Harris, *Notes from a Different Drummer; A Guide to Juvenile Fiction Portraying the Handicapped.* (New York: R.R. Bowker Company, 1977), p. 8.

at least, that is a word that for many is taboo. We have many more words to describe people at the younger end of the age spectrum than at the older end. Moreover, we seem to have a distinct lack of words that evoke positive, or even neutral, reactions.

Clearly, there are taboo and euphemistic words for aging. We are all getting older, but by and large our culture has not given us so many positive associations for the word *old*, except for certain material things such as recipes or antiques. It may be all right for a person to be *older*, but it is not all right to be called *old*. Ask friends what their word associations are for *old man* or *old woman*. Contrast those with *young man* or *young woman*. *Elderly* may be better, but some people who are so classified will object that it makes them feel too old, or it sounds like another euphemism for *sickly* or *infirm*.

The term *senior citizen* may serve as a general word, though as yet it may sound conspicuously euphemistic unless we also can speak of *junior citizens*. Younger Americans may think of *senior citizen* only as a category of people eligible for discounts on buses and at movie theatres. If shortened to *seniors* the word may come to sound *natural*. The Gray Panthers organization uses the term *super senior* now for people who are more than eighty, reminding others in the process that any single word is too abstract to identify people anywhere from sixty or sixty-five or one hundred or more.

And what do you hope to be called as you enter your *golden years*?

Summary

Subjects that we regard with fear, embarrassment, and usually ignorance, are likely to be given special treatment symbolically. We may avoid talking about a subject; we may react very strongly to certain words associated with the subject; we may seek to invent and use newer words that for awhile, at least, seem to allow us to talk more easily. In time, however, if our attitudes about the subject have not changed much, the euphemism is likely to provoke the same reaction as the word it was intended to replace.

Often our response is to deal with our feelings only at the level of words, seeking new euphemisms or more subtle circumlocutions. We might do better to explore the underlying reasons that give rise to our fears and embarrassment.

7

Creativity

The Goose in the Bottle

A constant theme in semantics literature is that we are often unnecessarily hindered by our semantic habits. Unable to see past certain labels or seemingly incapable of reacting to symbols in varied and flexible ways, we get snared in verbal webs that we ourselves have spun. But if language can impose its own limits, on our thinking and actions, then it seems equally capable of freeing us. The source of innovation, invention, creativity, or problem solving, no less than dreary habit and prejudice, can be the same: the symbols through which we encounter our world.

This philosophy is well expressed in an old Zen story. You have a large glass bottle with a long thin neck. Inside this bottle you have a slightly smaller goose, also with a long thin neck. How can you get the goose out of the bottle without breaking the bottle and without harming the goose?

Think about the question. We will consider the classic Zen answer later in the chapter, but perhaps by then several other answers equally creative will have suggested themselves to you.

What are some of the ways in which semantic habits block our thinking and actions? How might we be more flexible and creative in our behavior? Consider the following.

Over the line. Someone has written the letters of the alphabet in the following way. If you were to continue writing the letters, which would you place above the line, and which would you place below?

A   E F H I
————————————————
  B C D   G   J

There are several common reactions to this sort of problem. One is, "Oh, I'm not good at these problems"—a reaction that simultaneously labels oneself, pluralizes the problem into *these problems*, and puts *them* into an anonymous category. If you ask the person what kind are *these problems* the response may be the tautology, "The kind I'm not good at!" In any case, the chances of solving the problem are scarcely helped by the semantic double whammy that makes the problem seem harder and the person seem duller. Something very much like this affects millions of girls and young women in the United States every year. Taught in subtle ways that math is a subject for boys but not girls, many not only fail to learn what they are capable of, they also come to fear mathematics and related subjects. In response, many universities have instituted "math anxiety clinics," primarily for women. Once the students understand the basis of their fears and begin to reclassify themselves, their math ability makes a startling improvement.

This particular problem, however, is probably not one of *these problems*—assuming that a person had in mind some advanced problem in math or logic. The alphabet problem, however, has been used as part of an entrance examination for Japanese kindergartens. Given that information, the problem might be approached with a little less fear and the very simple pattern discovered: letters made with straight lines are written above the line, and those with curved lines are written below it.

Probably the most formidable block to solving many kinds of problems is labeling the problem or the would-be solver or both in such a way as to discourage all effort. Yet this is not the only semantic barrier.

If we are not restricted by classifications which limit our abilities, and if we can avoid labeling a kind of problem in such a way as to make its solution that much more difficult, we come upon perhaps the most widespread semantic limitation to problem solving and creativity. This is the narrow range of ways in which we classify that with which—or with whom—we must work. It is not only the sculptor who should be able to see the potentials of shaping the materials he or she works with. Managers, teachers, parents, even good friends often fail to see the potential of others whom they have restricted by a narrow set of classifications.

Over the years many experiments in creativity and problem solving have demonstrated the same principle, namely that limited and inflexible labeling of *things* prevents realization of their potential value. A classic experiment in problem solving was presented by Karl Duncker. He invited people into a room which, he said, was to be used for some visual experiments. In order to provide light for one of the experiments, the visitors were told three small candles needed to be mounted side by side, at eye level, on the door. The materials that might be used to accomplish this task are shown in the drawing. They include some sheets of paper, some paper clips, an ash tray, a small box of tacks, a small box of candles, and a box of matches. Before you read on, consider how you might attach those candles to the door at eye level?

In his initial experiment in the form described above, more than half the people who took part were unable to solve the problem. In a second version he made one significant change: he removed the tacks and the candles and the matches and left the empty cardboard boxes on the table. This time, everybody was able to solve the problem because the boxes were seen not

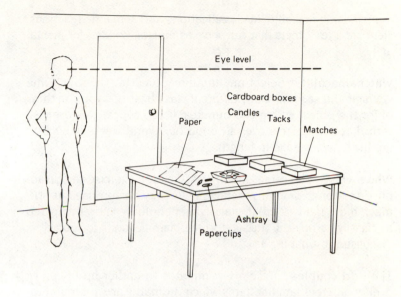

Eye level

Cardboard boxes

Candles

Paper

Tacks

Matches

Ashtray

Paperclips

as *containers* of other items but as resources for the task. In a third variation, he left the tacks, candles, and matches on the table and filled the boxes with buttons. Mentally classifying them as *boxes of buttons* and thus irrelevant, nearly 90 percent of those who were asked to solve the problem were unable to do so.

Many other experiments in problem solving have shown the same kind of connection between how something is classified and thus how it is perceived and regarded. Why is it that we are often less varied or imaginative in our classification schemes? There are no doubt many reasons, but there is surely social and cultural pressure that discourages playfulness, fantasy, and imagination that does not seem to be sufficiently serious or immediately practical. It is not surprising, then, that many psychologists have remarked that children are much more creative than adults. Artists, too, have expressed envy for the artistic creativity of children compared to adults whose experiences and skills may be admirable, but whose vision becomes narrower and more predictable in the process.

Some of the exercises described provide excellent practice

in increasing flexibility in classifications and semantic reactions. Here are a few others that can serve as *creativity isometrics* for mental agility.

Watchamacallit. Select any familiar object at random. Time yourself and see how many different classifications you can think of for the object within two minutes. If you repeat this exercise with different objects over a period of several weeks, your lists are likely to increase in length.

Who's what. The same kind of classification exercise can be applied to friends or family members. We may be surprised at how much more rigid we are in classifying people we know compared to classifying objects. (Recall, too the classifications for ourselves discussed in Chapter 3.)

The odd couples. Take a few minutes to gather up fifteen or twenty different familiar items which ordinarily are not found together—keys, a pencil, a sock, a carrot or onion, a nail; the more unrelated the better. Next put items together in pairs that strike you as totally unrelated, such as the keys and the carrot.

When you have formed all of the items into odd couples, write down as many explanations as you can of what the items in each pair have in common. Write until you cannot think of any more reasons and then go on to the next pair. You will find that this exercise helps you to abstract from the items and how they are symbolized in new, imaginative ways.

Some time after doing this exercise, you are likely to discover something else. You will remember the items, and how they were paired up together much better than if you had viewed them individually and also better than if you had grouped them in some *logical* arrangement.

Exercises in novel classifications such as this can do much to help increase our flexibility in viewing our environment and the people around us. However, if everybody began to group things as we did—keys and carrots—the combinations and the rationale that we devised would come to seem perfectly natural.

104

Just as a brilliant work of art can be reduced to such a cliché that the original loses its arresting quality, the same is true of any classification that becomes routine.

The pressures of tradition and restrictions of bureaucracies are notoriously rigid about classifications. Adhering to official policies, fitting each unique case into a fixed set of categories, the bureaucrat is spared the necessity of coming up with fresh ideas. Indeed, the very purpose and advantage of a rigid system lies in its standardization, its seeming imperviousness to individual variation. It is true that the indifference to the uniqueness of each individual or situation is more likely to be felt by one who feels he or she is a powerless victim of the system. For one on the inside—one who knows well that standarization is a kind of language itself—some creativity from within is possible.

Not all creative solutions to problems are appreciated or acceptable. Robert Benchley was one of America's most whimsical and creative humorists. While he was a student at Harvard, however, his "creative" answers were not always appreciated. On an economics final examination, Benchley was required to write a brief essay on the Massachusetts fishing industry from any point of view. He wrote his essay from the point of view of a fish. The instructor was not amused. Or perhaps he was, but Benchley was given failing grade.

Often we appear more conventional, less creative, in what we say or do because we fear that anything more original will be laughed at or criticized. In time we stop thinking in novel or unusual ways. Thus there often is a difference between problems and solutions posed in books or as experiments and those presented in everyday life where the *correct* or *best* answer depends, at least in part, on how well it is received by others.

Yet another limitation on innovative and creative ways of thinking is the concern with what others think of our ideas. When other people are with us (even if only in our thoughts), we usually monitor what we say. We do this for many reasons, including wanting to avoid giving offense or what we may regard as the wrong impression. In so doing we may withhold certain ideas we fear might be brushed aside or ridiculed.

It is to avoid such reactions that the technique popularly known as *brainstorming* is often used in groups trying to come up with new ideas. Brainstorming rules usually disallow any expression of disapproval of an idea when it is put forth. The hope is that any idea, no matter how crazy it might sound, should be heard. Even if an idea seems bizarre, it may influence others to think of something else which eventually may lead to the solution. Brainstorming also can reveal how rich and complex our semantic reactions are. One suggestion can evoke reactions in others based on any number of symbolic associations. You might try recording such a brainstorming session, and later try to follow the remarkable logic that connects the ideas.

Lower and Higher Level Abstractions

In Chapter 3 we discussed levels of abstraction, describing words that are closer to descriptions of sense data perceptions as *lower level abstractions*. Words that are either generalizations (like the word *people*) or concepts that cannot be described in sense data terms are called *high level abstractions*. Korzybski's philosophy distrusted higher level abstractions because the symbols represented concepts so far removed from the empirical world. He also wrote of the proper "order of abstracting," from lower to higher, from observation to greater abstraction. That same preference may be recommended for more creative thinking. The more we have abstracted from something, the less we really perceive it. Therefore, we may be less capable of viewing something from several different angles. Problems are often resolved much more easily when we can visualize them than when we talk about them. This is why we are so often encouraged to draw pictures or diagrams of problems we are working on. *Looking at* may be more efficient than *thinking about*.

Consider this simple problem:

A hungry book worm decides to eat her way though a three volume set of encyclopedias which are arranged on a shelf in their normal order. Being a meticulous book worm, she decides to eat from page 1 of Volume I, and stop on the last page of Volume III. The cover of each volume is ¼ inch thick (¼ inch for the front cover, ¼ inch for the back cover), and the pages of each volume are two inches thick. How far will this hungry book worm travel, following her plan and following the shortest route from page 1 of Volume I to the last page of Volume III?

When people "think about" this problem, they usually add front and back cover for each volume (¼ + ¼ = ½), plus 2 inches for the pages of each volume, and multiply by three inches for a total of seven and one-half inches. Then they subtract the ¼ inch from Volume I and ¼ inch from Volume III and come up with 7 inches.

People who draw, however, are likely to arrive at a different number. Why? When we draw a picture or a diagram, we are more likely to notice details that may be important than if we merely imagine the object. A drawing, while still an abstraction, is at a lower level of abstraction than the image conjured up by the word alone. For the case of the encyclopedias, draw the three volumes arranged on a shelf in the usual order. Now ask yourself, where is page one of Volume I, and where is the last page of Volume III? How far will our friend, the book worm, travel?

Definitions

To indicate how a word is to be used, we sometimes present a definition. Defining something narrows its range and sets limits. Not only words may be defined. Sociologists and those in communication also speak of *definitions of situations*. A classroom, for example, may be defined in several different ways by different students. For one, the classroom may be a place where the teacher speaks and the students listen and write down what the teacher says. For another student, the classroom may be a place for the exchange of ideas between students and the teacher. Still another student may define a particular classroom as a kind of minefield to try to cross without getting blown away in the effort. Each definition of the situation will influence how the student acts and how the student interprets the actions of others.

Perhaps in defining situations we are so concerned with figuring out which definition is socially desirable that we fail to be more imaginative or creative.

My wife was once discouraged about looking for a job in a new city. She defined herself as a capable, experienced professional woman, and resented the kind of treatment she received when she entered an employment agency. There she seemed to be defined as just one more unemployed applicant. After two or three uncomfortable experiences, she decided she would redefine the situation. When she entered the next agency she turned things around. Approaching the receptionist in a more positive manner, she briefly explained that she was not looking for a job. She was, she said, looking for the most appropriate agency in the city for a person of her background and qualifications. She quickly found herself talking with the manager of the agency, interviewing him rather than being interviewed, and having the manager try to impresss her with the agency's background and qualifications. She had redefined the situation and in the process raised her own spirits, altered her own behavior, and learned a good deal of useful information.

Persons whom society has labeled *handicapped* or *disadvantaged* (see Chapter 5) are often far more *creative* than are those who are not so labeled and hence may be less aware of their particular limitations. Persons who are handicapped often say their biggest handicap is not their physical condition but the social restrictions that result from being labeled handicapped by others. Often required to work around the physical or symbolic structures that serve others, such people are extraordinarily creative in redefining their situation in order to make their way in society.

We might, in fact, all be more creative in how we see our-selves and others if we could experience the world from the point of view of one with a physical disability. Such is the point of view of Victoria Ann-Lewis, who with three other *disabled* women put together a delightful and witty musical revue. Their reclassifi-cations appear in the title "Tell Them I'm a Mermaid," and in songs throughout, such as "Don't You Wish You Could be Dis-abled?" Says Nancy Becker Kennedy who has had to use a wheel-chair since she broke her neck in an automobile accident, "You're going to think this is nuts, but becoming disabled is a marvelous thing to go through. Even if a lot of it is hideous, it's a privilege, really like an odyssey to Hell and back . . . . If everybody could do it and come out able-bodied, I'd really recommend it."[1]

Ambiguous Language

A word or phrase may be interpreted in more than one way. The context in which the expression appears—including the verbal context but also the subject matter, occasion, speaker, and lis-tener—usually narrows the meaning sufficiently to reduce the range of possible interpretations.

Sometimes, however, a word or phrase is deliberately in-tended to have more than one meaning. Often the intention is to show humor or wit. This is true in much of modern print ad-vertising (as you can see by glancing at almost any full page magazine ad). It also can be seen in t-shirt messages, bumper sticker messages, and in many jokes—especially suggestive jokes. In many cases the ambiguity allows one to say one thing that might seem innocent enough, while suggesting something else. The "funny" part is when we, make that second connection. We see this type of language in those comic signs posted in bars

[1]Tom Shales, " 'Mermaid' Adeptly Raises Consciousness," *Albuquerque Journal* (Dec. 4, 1983), p. A-11

and restaurants: "IF YOU THINK YOUR WAITER IS RUDE YOU SHOULD SEE OUR MANAGER" or "SPILLED DRINKS CAN RUN INTO MONEY."

Many popular puzzles and riddles and more sophisticated verbal problems may be solved by virtue of the ambiguity of expression. Those who are stumped are those who fail to see another interpretation: Those who solve the problem are, to some extent, open to the multiple meanings of expressions.

Here are a couple of problems of this kind. Solutions are given at the end of the chapter.

- In the year 1955, how many months had 28 days?
- Charles Brown is Dr. Leslie Brown's son, but Dr. Leslie Brown is not Charles Brown's father. How is this possible?

R-Thinking and A-Thinking

Some psychologists distinguish between two broad types of thinking. One kind is *reality adjusted thinking* or *R-thinking*. This is the sort of thinking involved in the analysis of complex information and in problem solving. Korzybskian general semantics is concerned almost exclusively with R-thinking, with the guiding principle that our language must be adjusted to the objective realities it represents.

There is another kind of thinking which is sometimes called *autistic thinking* or *A-thinking*. As the name may suggest, this is mental activity which is very private and not primarily adjusted to "reality." Dreaming is one kind of A-thinking. Day-dreaming is another. So are hypnagogic states, hallucinations, and other mental work and mental play.

One form of A-thinking is eidetic imagery. This is mental imagery that seems as if it were real. That is, a person is able mentally to project an image that may have the appearance or sound or odor of something "real." What is curious is that an

estimated ninety percent of children have this ability, while perhaps only ten percent of adults are able to experience eidetic
images. The reasons for this loss of ability are unclear. They may
relate to the changes in the brain that occur around puberty.
(Learning a second or third language is far more difficult after
that time primarily due to the lateralization of the brain, not because one is otherwise too old.) The reasons are also likely to
be related to the overwhelming reliance on words as we negotiate
our way though life. At some point we stop *seeing* things, and start
reading them. Or, with music, people stop listening and start labeling—music group, name of music, type of music, and so forth.

While teaching in Japan, I knew students who were skillful
with the *soroban*, or Japanese *abacus*, which is still widely used
throughout Asia as the basic calculator in shops, banks, and at
home. Some students were able to visualize an abacus and also
visualize sliding the beads up and down the rods, performing the
calculations. Such a person could easily *see* the answer to math
problems most of us could not possibly work in our heads (such
as $47 \times 13 - 8 = 603$).

There is a case reported of a student who was taking a final
examination and could not remember a particular quote she
wanted to mention. She could remember where she had read the
quotation, however. She envisioned herself leaving the classroom,
going to the library, finding the book in the stacks, thumbing
through the book to the right page, and then reading the quote,
which she wrote down word for word in her blue book. She later
said she felt a little guilty for "cheating."

Among the best known persons gifted with the ability for all
kinds of eidetic experiences was Cornell's Professor Titchner, one
of the school's most celebrated scholars and eloquent lecturers.
With his eidetic abilities, Titchner could lecture in great detail
without any need for lecture notes.

Synaesthesia is another form of A-thinking which is more
widespread than some others. Synaesthesia refers to the mixing
or joining of different sensory experiences. We sometimes talk
as if we mix senses, such as using a word associated with sound
to describe something that is visual. We may speak of *loud colors*,

for example. We often use thermal terms with other senses—*cool jazz* or *warm textures*. But as a kind of A-thinking, synaesthesia actually mixes sensory experiences. Many people have strong color associations with certain numbers, or with days of the week (not counting idioms or clichés, such as blue Monday). In Japan, synaesthesia is basic to the aesthetics and everyday life of the culture. The familiar wind chime (*furin*), for example, is just a little bell with a large tag attached to the clapper so that the wind will make the bell ring. The idea is that on a hot summer day when you hear the gentle sound of the *furin* you will *feel* the breeze that caused it to ring and therefore feel cooler. That certain colors make one feel warmer or cooler is another example of a kind of synaesthesia.

Creativity should employ all the human resources. Problems are usually defined in R-thinking terms and perhaps are best solved in R-thinking ways. This means not being misled or blocked by words. It may also mean being as flexible as possible in classifying what we are working with, and how we define a situation. But A-thinkimg needs to be encouraged, too. To dismiss daydreaming or other interior experiences as idle can snuff out the first flickers of creativity.

Oh, yes. In the year 1955, as in every year, all months had 28 days. And, Dr. Leslie Brown is Charles Brown's mother. Now, as to the goose in the bottle: ask yourself how it got into the bottle in the first place? Well, you *said* it was in the bottle. So, how can we get it out? . . .

8

Organizing
Our
Experience

Remember that great year at Plainfield State Teacher's College
when the football team chalked up so many victories it was ranked
nationally among the top small college teams that were untied
and undefeated? Remember the team's great quarterback, Johnny
Chung, who would down a bowl of rice between the halves and
come out to lead Plainfield on to victory and an invitation to the
coveted Blackboard Bowl? No? Maybe you are too young to remember, for it was over thirty years ago when Plainfield State
was part of the Saturday night football results. And just as well,
too, because there was no such college as Plainfield State. It was
all a hoax, later described by Alexander Klein in *Grand Deception*,
devised by a New Jersey public relations man who was over-
whelmed by the Saturday night litany of football scores which
seemed to come mostly from places he'd never been and didn't
really care to know about. The Plainfield eleven would have gone
on to that glorious Blackboard Bowl, too, if *Time* magazine hadn't
wanted to do a story on the team and their fabled quarterback
Chung. Caught at last, the final news release described how the

team, including Johnny, was all caught cheating on an exam, and the ball game was over.

Most of what we read about or hear about on radio or television concerns people we've never seen, places we've never visited, and events that may or may not ever happen. In the sports stories that year, Plainfield State Teacher's College of Plainfield, New Jersey, had as much symbolic reality as Notre Dame or Slippery Rock. It wasn't until somebody checked up that they found there was no such school, that it was all a hoax. If that amuses you and you feel better for knowing about it, how do you know that this story and Alexander Klein and all that is not yet another hoax?

In this chapter we are not interested in the intentionally distorted expressions—like hoaxes, exaggerations, or lies (another interesting example of labeling)—but rather with the well-intentioned, most common statements we make and hear every day. We would like to be able to set forth some standards or criteria for evaluating what we say on the basis of its reliability, to be able to know *how* we know what we're talking about. We would like to allow for all kinds of expressions and yet be able to discriminate among them: to know the difference, for example, between what some would call a *fact* and what some would call a *hunch*; and between what nobody can dispute because it is personal judgment; and statements that almost all of us agree on because, without knowing it, we have already agreed to agree.

We will begin with what seems to be a basic distinction.

A Double Standard: Sense Data and System

It is important to distinguish between two procedures for evaluating symbols: (1) the testing of a symbol against the nonverbal *sense-data reality*; and (2) the testing of a symbol within a *system of other symbols*. The sentence, "Does this dog have fleas?" may be answered by examining the nonverbal dog. The sentence,

114

"Does this dog have a soul?" may be answered, not by examining the dog, but by studying the way in which the word *soul* is used within some religious system. To examine the dog to discover his soul or to discuss in the abstract a question like, "Does this dog have fleas?" is to confuse the two standards and thus to render any decision meaningless. When we fail to recognize the words may be tested against either standard, or when we confuse the two in the proces of evaluation, our thinking will be confused.

These two standards for evaluation provide the two basic traditions and methods in philosophy and science, as well as in everyday behavior. There is a *sense-data orientation* (at the lowest levels of abstraction and often called the *extensional orientation* in the semantics of Korzybski), and there is a *system orientation* (at the higher levels of abstraction, with or without an awareness of the process of abstracting, and sometimes called by the semanticists an *intensional orientation*.) In reasoning, the inductive method begins with the sense data and moves toward a systemization of it; the deductive method begins with the system and draws conclusions about sense data from the rules of the system.

We find the contrasting orientations of *sense-data emphasis vs.* an emphasis on systems to be a convenient way to compare competing trends in the varied fields of education, philosophy, political theory, religion, and others. The classical education in the Western world, for example, for centuries stressed "the seven liberal arts." Modern liberal arts colleges have long since strayed from the original seven disciplines, of course. But those original seven (rhetoric, grammar, logic, mathematics, geometry, music, and astronomy) were severely system oriented. All were concerned with learning the rules of the systems; the first three, the *Trivium*, were primarily verbal systems, the latter four, the *Quadrivium*, were primarily numerical. Astronomy was the only subject that sounds *scientific*, but by studying the stars and planets—instead of plants and animals—one was seeking to discover the "eternal system" of a reality safely distant from the prying hands of curious students. More comtemporary fields in education—the natural and social sciences, field studies, and so on, are, in contrast, far more sense-data oriented.

Deductive reasoning, formal logic, mathematics, and a prescriptive approach to human behavior, including language, is primarily system oriented. Induction, empiricism pragmatism, and a descriptive approach to human behavior (how people act and talk, not how the rules say people should) is more sense-data oriented. Similarly, the distinction between conservative philosophies in religion and politics, with an emphasis on retaining the traditional social or moral order, leans toward the system side. Liberalism in its many forms in religion or politics stresses change, process, and challenges to "the system."

An obvious parallel exists between the two orientations of *sense data* and *systems* in the relationship of perceived *reality* and language. No two things in the world, it is said, are exactly alike: this is the lesson of the snowflakes. But we use the same words, over and over, for identifying things that are not really identical. Would it be possible to imagine a language where every word was different in order, in some way to symbolize the awareness of the differences of things? The answer seems to be *no*. If every utterance were unique we would have no basis for imitating and hence learning a language and no basis for comprehension. In short, we would have no *system*, no language.

In the history of philosophy we find many thinkers who have emphasized the *system orientation* and others who have emphasized the sense-data orientation. F. S. C. Northrop has suggested that the former has characterized Western thought and that the latter has characterized Eastern thought.[1] Even Northrop's distinction might be regarded by some Eastern philosophers as essentially Western, since it is so neatly two-valued (but maybe most would agree with him anyway).

But we do not have to pit West against East to illustrate the basic difference. Western philosophy has had its share of thinkers who have emphasized the system orientation and those who have emphasized sense data. This is particularly true in the Anglo-American tradition, for much as Americans may pay homage to

---

[1] F. S. C. Northrop, *The Meeting of East and West* (New York: Macmillan, 1946).

the genius of ancient Greece, American thought owes more to England and a very different empirical tradition. For purposes of illustration and simplification, consider the alternative philosophies of Plato and of Francis Bacon, the last of the Rennaisance men and the first of "the moderns."

Plato distrusted sense data because it was fleeting, differed from person to person, and was therefore unsound. His desire for something so permanent that it was eternal, unchanging, and everywhere the same represents what is sometimes called *the classical attitude*. In his *Theatetus*, for example, he presents what might have been a description of transactional perception such as was presented in the previous chapter of this book. However, instead of making the point that people see things differently, Plato makes the point that *because* perception is so complex, we must distrust it. For something more reliable, Plato moved to a system that was not of this world of sense, but of an *ideal* world where such problems did not exist. A Platonist of this century, Richard Weaver, states the position clearly.

> Naturally, everything depends on what we mean by knowledge. I shall adhere to the classic proposition that there is no knowledge at the level of sensation, that therefore knowledge is of universals, and that whatever we know as a truth enables us to predict. The process of learning involves interpretation, and the fewer particulars we require in order to arrive at our generalization, the more apt pupils we are in the school of wisdom.
>
> The whole tendency of modern thought, one might say its whole moral impulse, is to keep the individual busy with endless induction, Since the time of Bacon the world has been running away from, rather than toward, first principles, so that, on the verbal level, we see "fact" substituted for "truth," and on the philosophical level, we witness attack upon abstract ideas and speculative inquiry.[2]

[2]Richard Weaver, *Ideas Have Consequences*(Chicago: University of Chicago Press, 1948, 1960), pp. 12–13.

117

Such a view may be comforting, but it binds us to other symbolic systems. Weaver, like Plato we might assume, is extremely distrustful of our attempts to appraise what we call *reality*. (Reality is at the sense-data level, where triangles are never quite perfect, circles never exactly round, and descriptions at best only approximate expectations based on theory.) In short, the system orientation which we have tried to illustrate through Plato and a modern-day Platonist, Weaver, regards human perception of sense data as failing the elegance and consistency possible only in some symbolic system.

Francis Bacon represents the opposite view. His writings, which in so many ways anticipated by four hundred years, the ideas of contemporary semanticists, reveal a nearly total distrust of *systems* and an equally total faith in sense data. Bacon argued for *pure induction*, by which he meant the careful cataloguing of sense data until one had a sufficient sampling of examples to move to something more general. The system would grow naturally but slowly. Before we could formulate a theory of *heat* or *light*, for example, we would have to take all known instances of heat or light and study them. And then we could begin to generalize, to elaborate a system.

Neither view is satisfactory. A system that would disregard our daily experiences is of limited utility. And besides, we should ask where such a system came from before we accept it.[3] A system based purely on inducted sense data is impossible, for before we can use the terms *heat* or *light* we have to assume that they belong to some system. What do we include and what do we exclude? In both systems we find the ignorance of language as a human invention that has evolved through accident and convention, not design.

The way we interpret everyday experiences and the tradition of the scientific method both require combinations of system and sense data. To begin with incidents in our personal lives we may say that we have few experiences that do not involve, in

[3]Often the explanation of total systems is that they are *inspired* and therefore preferable to our own modest ideas.

different degrees, both sense data and an accepted system By *experience* I mean all of the attitudes, anticipations, and so on, that come into play whenever we perceive something. To take a pleasant example, a kiss is something more than sense data. If one reflects on the event, as persons have been known to do, what one means when he or she says, "I have been kissed" is not just the recollection of tactile senses, but something much more complex. It is an experience that involves the system in which a kiss has some significance (love or respect or betrayal) but something that is not *just* some verbal classification of the meaning of a kiss.

Or, if one observes that it is raining, the experience is not just sense data. If it were, the description would be completely different if one were inside looking out from what it would be if one were standing in the rain. The sense data are different in each case. Inside, one could see something, or hear something or smell something. Outside, one might feel something, or smell something, or one might or might not see something. Why call both by the same name *rain*? To observe that it is raining is an interpretation that goes beyond any sense data, for the idea of *rain* is part of a system that has organized a whole constellation of experiences into the classification *rain*.

It is difficult to pass a day and maintain a total sense-data orientation or a total system orientation. As we try to make our experiences meaningful we move from one orientation to the other. Nor, or course, are the two positions as neat and fixed as this discussion might indicate.

The attitude of the semanticist tends to distrust verbal systems that would limit our experience or alter the nonverbal world to fit the verbal world. Life experiences should be served by language, and not the other way around. To this extent (and in this direction) the semanticist is sense-data oriented.

To summarize for now, let us say that all experience is a combination of immediate sense data that is given meaning within a larger system. The system may be the system of language by which we determine and classify some event. Or the system may be religious or political or social, by which we interpret the event. In the first case, it is cultural and linguistic and unavoidable; in the second, it is more personal and, to some extent, a matter of choice. With sense data only, we can go nowhere (if indeed we can have sense data only when we grow up in a society and learn a language before we are conscious of it). With system only we are hyperinterpretive, overly linguistic, or "hung up" on words and systems. What is important is the point at which we begin and emphasize. The directives provided by the previous chapter indicate that we are safer if we start with the *experience*, as close to the sence data as we can be.

Mature and Premature Organization of Experience

Every day we have occasion to place events into some system that seems to work for us. If it is a cold winter morning and the car doesn't start the first time or the second time or the third time, we must decide whether it will start the fourth time (or *n*th time) or whether we should take the bus. At the time of the decision we trust a system based on past experiences. We move from the extensional experience to the intensional interpretation ("Eventually this car will start" or, "This car will never start"). When to do this is unpredictable. Or, it is predictable only within a range of probability. If you were totally system oriented, you would know what would happen before you tried. If you were purely inductive you would never quite know.

Often, we make judgments of other people on the basis of the *results* of their systems or lack of them. "Some people don't know when to quit," we say of the fool. "Some people have what it takes," we say of the hero. Now, the fool and the hero may be the same person—but the hero has tried one more time.

Greek mythology is filled with characters who are extravagantly extensional, though more through punishment than com-

120

pulsion or fortitude.[4] Sisyphus and Tantalus come to mind immediately. Their efforts are will continuing, so far as we know. We may feel hope or pity or, since Camus and the existentialists, identification toward them. If we are "in on the mythology," we know that the fruits and drink for Tantalus will always be just out of reach, and that Sisyphus never had a chance either. But we can say this only about others, for it is their choice, not ours, whether or not to try again, whether or not to make a general conclusion (a system). When it is our choice we know that we don't know for sure. We tend to act in predictable behavior, it is true, not because anything is inevitable but because, in classical terms, we become products of our own mythology. In this sense, the faithful who never gives up and the neurotic who always gives up are not so different except in the label we give them. Our own lives are spent in that vast land in between.

There are many instances in which our prediction of what will happen (our classification of some experience into a system) is influential in determining what does happen. Such instances we discussed in Chapter 5. But to the extent that "the world is independent of our will" we have to make guesses. What guesses we make will depend, in part, on how we describe the world in the first place.

Ordinary Language

In order to record or communicate our experiences, we reduce those experiences to symbols that can be popularly understood. Because these symbols must be negotiable within the

---

[4]This is one explanation for classical Greek punishment. As in Greek tragedy, the idea of inevitability (system) is crucial in the cruel Greek punishment. Perhaps in our day in which probability, not certainty, is the rule, our attitude toward the punishment is different.

whole society that speaks our language, our symbolic expressions of experiences are necessarily "loose," even sloppy. Language is never precise, for its very nature and purpose require it to be more general than any single experience that might be described in the language. This *ordinary language* conveys the bulk of our symbolized experience. A scientist or specialist in any field demands a more precise language, for those who read or hear his or her words are a smaller population with special training in the language.

Moreover, since language is a product of man, there is something of man in all of his statements—even those that seem to be statements about the "outside" world. As we noted before, when one moves from sense data to experience, the degree of personal involvement increases considerably, and most of our meaningful expressions are about *experiences* of one kind or another. There are degrees of personal involvement in statements about the outside world, however. The enthusiastic drunk who praises his performing elephants or the child who complains to his parents about the billion tigers in his bedroom or the D student who stands in the rain looking at his first A paper and exclaims, "it is a beautiful day!" are very much a part of what they presume to describe. But though these examples are extreme, the difference is the one of degree. Whenever we say anything we put something of us into what we describe. Even though our ordinary language is less than precise, we can still make important distinctions among kinds of sentences. These provide standards for evaluation that are very important if we are to use our language as best we can. For example, we may distinguish among the following sentences:

1. *The dog is barking.*
2. *The dog is healthy.*
3. *The dog is man's best friend.*
4. *The "dog" is a four-legged animal that barks.*

All of the above sentences begin with the same three words. All use a common subject, *the dog*, followed by the ubiquitous and, in English, ambiguous verb *is*. And yet, each sentence, if we imagine a probable context, is different. The first is a sentence of description, the second is a sentence based on inference, the third is a value judgment, and the fourth is a tautology. These four sentence types probably encompass most of our ordinary conversation. We shall examine these one at a time.

Statements of Description

If we have a dog before us and the dog is barking, we should be able to agree on the statement, "The dog is barking." If we were all deaf, we might be able to see the dog open and close its mouth but not tell whether the dog was barking or not. ("I see it open and close its mouth, but I hear nothing—is it barking?") As the word *barking* is usually used, it refers to sound. To make a statement about sound we must be capable of perceiving such sound.

Likewise, if we could not observe the dog, we would have no basis for our agreement. Suppose, for example, we know from experience that when the phone rings in Barney's apartment, his dog barks wildly. Our idea of a good time is to telephone Barney's apartment and know that his dog will begin barking when the phone rings. We may agree that Barney's dog is barking when we telephone, but because we cannot *observe* the dog our agreement may not be justified.

The most accurate statements are those made about the observed by persons capable of observation. Because of the limitations of any single individual, the more persons who can observe and agree about their observations, the more trust we can put into their common statements of description. Agreement alone is not a sufficient criterion for putting trust into a statement. There are many ways of producing agreement in society, from the subtle pressures of habit, Fromm's "anonymous authority," "common sense," and so on, to more obvious forms of overt coercion.[5]

We will call those statements made about the observed *by more than one person* capable of making the observations statements of *description*. By these standards, then, statment number one, if made about a dog we have observed barking, is a statement of description.

Statements of Inference

Suppose we have that dog before us and one of us says, "The dog is healthy." We have something to observe (the dog doing something), but can we observe the *health* in the way that we could observe the *barking*? The adjective *healthy* is usually applied to some internal condition that cannot be observed. We often qualify the word in a sentence, when it applies especially to us, with "I think I am" or "I feel" because we cannot observe all of the internal conditions that make up the description *healthy*, in a way that a doctor might. (When we visit the doctor or take our dog to the veterinarian we are seeking to test our inference.)

Now you can imagine various observable actions that might indicate that the dog is healthy, but because you cannot observe the internal condition that is the ordinary-language meaning of *healthy*, you cannot call this sentence a statement of description. As with the first sentence which was made without having observed the dog, we are making a guess about the unknown on the basis of the known. Such statements we will call *statements of inference*.

Statements of inference may be ranked according to their ability to be verified after they have been made. The range of

[5]For those who feel that agreement alone is proof of anything, remedial reading in Hans Christian Andersen's "The Emperor's New Clothes" is recommended.

verification runs from *immediately verifiable* to *unverifiable*. If you telephone a friend and make the inference, "My friend should be home at this hour, and therefore I infer that he will answer the telephone," you may determine whether your inference was correct within a matter of seconds. If, however, your phone rings, and when you pick it up there is nobody on the other end of the line, you may make the inference that a prankster has called you and never be able to verify who telephoned you or why.

Statements of inference may also be ranked according to their probability. Some guesses about the unknown are better guesses than others because some are based on more information or experience than others. Professional gamblers, insurance companies, and investors in the stock market are among those who "play the odds" by making the best inferences they can.

Statements of description are certain at the time of the observation; statements of inference ar probable and possibly verifiable at a later time.

Many writers prefer to distinguish among the variety of sentences that will pass for our category of *inferential statements*. A hypothesis that explains *why* something happened, and a guess about something that *will* happen might be separated. That is, a statement that explains a principle of why something happens in general (such as a law in physics), and a statement of prediction of a particular event made on the basis of that law might be distinguished. For most conversation, I do not believe that this distinction is essential. If I say that when I blow on this match flame the flame will go out, I am making a prediction about a future event on the basis of past events. My explanation may be inferentially based on certain laws of physics, that are presumed to explain the phenomenon. Or, my explanation may be a descriptive generalization of past events—all of the other times I have blown on matches they have gone out. In either case, when we make a guess about the unknown on the basis of the known, we are in the realm of inference, whether the guess is a plausible explanation or a guess about a specific future event.

Probably most human behavior operates on the basis of inference. This is true not only because any fool can spin out inferences but because most of the time we just do not have the facts on which to base our behavior. To make sense of what we do and to anticipate what we should do in the future, we must make assumptions. To recognize this does not mean that we may therefore abandon caution entirely. On the contrary, it means that we must be especially careful of these inferences, noting those that are more or less probable, recognizing the base of fact-description that supports the inferences. And we must be willing to alter our guesses when new information comes along.

Statements of Judgment

In the third statement in our list of four, "man's best friend" is not descriptive of anything that can be observed. It may be something of an inference based on what one man has felt (Barney's best friend *is* his dog), but others could make equally appropriate statements—"The dog is man's worst friend," for example. For statements of this kind, we bring into consideration our values. For one person a best friend is a dog; for another, a cat or canary; for another it might be his mother. Agreement proves little, because one is agreeing on values, not on observation. Such statements we will call *statements of judgment*[6]

Chacun a son goût is the accepted judgment about judgments-To each his own. You like your steaks well done, I like mine rare. You prefer the quarter system, I prefer the semester system. You are bored by this book, I think it's tremendous. *Chacun a son goût*.

The question of value, as Charles Morris has noted, cuts across all academic disciplines. Everybody has something to say

---

[6]You should note that we are using *judgment in the sense of value judgment*, and not in the sense in which the word is popularly used. In its common usage, *judgment* includes statements that we have called inferential—"I judge him to be over six feet tall"—in which case there is no preference stated about one's height.

about the nature of good or evil, and there is something to learn from everybody. But we can expect less agreement among statements of judgment than among statements of description or inference. We can expect more agreement at an international congress of physicists than we can among an international congress of epicures or critics.

It might be argued that judgments are often valuable because no agreement is required or even expected. It is this range of preferences among mankind that reveals and motivates the great variety of human behavior and its cultural artifacts. If we were all of the same judgment, we should all love the same person, desire the same diet, and demand the same occupation. Although this is not the case, fortunately, it is true that within a culture preferences do appear to be similar. Standards of beauty, fashion, pleasure, and so on, are learned in the same way that one's language is learned. To the extent that judgments are similar within a culture, judgments may be confused with descriptions. When everybody agrees about something it is easy for everybody to assume it must be true.

We would do well to recognize judgments for what they are and not expect or demand uniformity of judgment. What is important is to realize when we are making judgments, to avoid stating judgments as if they were facts, and to be open to other choices. Such an attitude not only improves the climate for communication and understanding, it also may make each of us a more interesting person.

Tautologies

The fourth statement about the dog is different still. We can observe the four legs, we can observe the barking. But let us assume that the sentence was not said in a way that meant that *this* dog has four legs (count'em) and is barking, but that *dog* is an animal that has four legs and barks. When we are talking about *dog*, we are talking about a word and how we wish to use it. We are giving a kind of definition of *dog*, however useful that definition may be. In the same way, we may say that "man is a featherless biped"; we are not saying that *this* man has no feathers and walks on two feet. We are saying that we may define *man* (and *kangaroo*, for that matter) in terms of these characteristics. Such definitions of *dog* and *man* may be utterly useless; in any case, they are definitions and not statements of description.

Agreement about the meaning or use of words is the characteristic of a *tautology*. When one tests the accuracy of a statement not by checking it against an observed reality (description) or against an unobserved but probable event or explanation (inference) or against one's value system (judgment) but rather against a system of usage, one has a tautology. Thus, the previous sentence is also a tautology—for it tells how the author wishes to use these words. When, *by definition*, "a dog is . . ." or "justice is . . ." or "nonsense is . . ." the statement is a tautology and cannot be proved but only accepted or rejected within a system of usage.

It is possible, therefore, to classify the third sentence ("The dog is man's best friend") as a tautology, if by the sentence one seeks to define *dog* in terms of friendship. Probably this is the most common meaning of that sentence, anyway, since persons utter the sentence without reference to the nonverbal world of dogs biting children and mailmen.

Possibly because the verb *is* in English is required to do so much work and is used in so many senses, statements originally meant as statements of inference or judgment come to be used as tautologies. By sheer repetition of one man's preference for dogs the English-speaking world comes to define *dog* in terms of a value system.

Conversation becomes confused and communication breakdowns occur when different classifications of statements become confused. Under the pressure of an argument or because of linguistic ambiguities one may start with one meaning of a sentence and retreat to another. What often happens is that a speaker begins with an assertion that seems like a description but is extended so far as to be a generalization. When this speaker is challenged he changes his description into a tautology in order to rule out any exception. For example, one person may assert that "women are emotional and never calm in the face of a crisis." Another person replies that he knows a woman who is less emotional and more relaxed in a crisis than most men. The first speaker replies, "Well, that person isn't *really* a woman." He has, in effect, switched from talking about women to talking about his definition of women. This very argument, of course, frequently appeared in a variety of forms by critics of the Women's Liberation movement, with many of the "spokespeople" for the movement being reclassified by their critics as something other than women.

One final distinction is important. When one says of a chess game, "the bishop moves diagonally on his own color as far as the players wishes or until stopped by another chesspiece," the person may be indicating a tautology or may be stating a description of what he has seen in a chess game. What is important to determine here is the circumstances that prompted the statement. Two possibilities are suggested. Was the statement made on the basis of observation or on the basis of reading a book on chess? If the first is the case, then the statement is a description, and as a description it has no validity beyond that description. That is, under such circumstances the speaker can only state inferences about how the bishop will move in the future, for he must make a guess about the unknown on the basis of the known. If the second is the case, the speaker needs no observation in order to talk about the past, present and the future, for he has *defined* the bishop in terms of its moves. Any piece that does not move in accordance with this definition is not a bishop. Under the latter conditions the statement is a tautology.

Standards and Contexts

It is risky at best to attempt to classify any given statement as a description, inference, judgment, or tautology unless one knows the context in which it appears. (Fortunately, statements rarely appear in isolation —except, perhaps, on some teachers' examination questions.) We will say more about some aspects of context in the next chapter, but for now we should note the general problem of evaluating statements in isolation.

At the very least, there is the verbal context, the other sentences in which a statement for evaluation is embedded; this is what people usually seem to have in mind when they object to being quoted "out of context." More than that, however, there are the paralinguistic markers (mentioned in the next chapter) that make the exclamation "good luck!" a cheerful wish when said one way and a sarcastic doubting of success when said in a different tone of voice. With written words out of verbal context it is impossible to know if the intention is one of encouragement or sarcasm. Then there is the context of time. What is an inference at one time may, at another time, be a statement of description. Most person would probably like to classify the statement, "The earth is round" (or "The earth is a spheroid") as a statement of fact-description, and yet the measures that would enable that statement to meet the appropriate standards are quite recent. The social and cultural context should be considered, too. There are probably different intentions when a theologian or a geographer observes that in every life a little rain must fall.

Apart from such broad contexts, we must also consider the specific conditions under which any statement is made, for these will have to be tested against our standards in order to evaluate the statement. The statement, "It is raining," for example, is a statement of description only if one has had experience observing the weather. If the statement is made only on the basis of hearing what sounds like thunder and a noise that sounds like water plopping on the roof, the sentence is an inference based on these experiences. The more precise speaker would say, "I hear what sounds like thunder and what sounds like water on the roof, and so I infer that it is raining." If this sounds picayune it may be because it would seem that usually no harm would come from guessing it was raining when it was not. But in most of our lives we must *act on inferences*, not on descriptions. At such times knowing we are making inferences might make us more cautious. To say, "The right turn signal on the car in front of me is blinking [description] and so I infer that he will turn [inference]" should make us more cautious about acting than if we say "the car in front of me is going to turn" as if our inference had the accuracy of a description.

One way to develop a keener critical attitude toward evaluating statements is to imagine a variety of contexts and specific conditions which might have provoked any one statement. Although in one sense this is working backward, using our imagination on sample statements can prepare us to be more critical of our own speaking habits and those of others. Consider the following examples and for each try to imagine different contexts, different conditions under which each statement might be made, resulting in different evaluations (and classifications) for each.

1. Nice guys finish last.
2. All roads lead to Rome.
3. February is the coldest month.
4. Coke is the pause that refreshes.
5. Lincoln: a great man, a great car!

Variations on the Theme

There are useful variations on the four kinds of sentences we have been discussing. Because the titles are descriptive, little explanation will be given.

Personal descriptions (*or to-me facts*): "I have a toothache" or "I

131

am sleepy." Here, verification by more than one observer is difficult or impossible.

Reports of descriptions: "The capital of Tibet is Lhasa"; "George Washington was born in 1732." The tests of descriptions have been met by qualified observers, but the person making the statement may not have been able to make the tests.

Reports of inferences: "There is no life on the planet Mars"; "Lee Harvey Oswald was mentally deranged"; "Patrick Henry said, 'Give me liberty or give me death.' " The first statement is, at this date, only an inference based on the best evidence; in the future, such a statement may be proven or disproven. The second statement poses several problems, including the inference that Oswald shot President Kennedy ("legal proof" by the Warren Commission puts the guilt of Oswald "beyond a reasonable doubt," though such proof has not been accepted universally). Another difficulty with the sentence is the meaning of "mentally deranged." For some, any person who shoots another is "mentally deranged"—this being one possible definition for mental derangement. If one takes other definitions, this condition can only be inferential. The third sentence is popularly thought to be a report of a description. But a little investigation will show that our record of the speech is one that first appeared in Henry's biography written twenty years later. One may infer that the famous phrase was composed not by Henry but by this biographer.

These four choices appear to extend along a linear continuum, with one pole represented by statements of description and the other representing tautologies. We might then place inferences next to statements of description, and put statements of judgment between the inferences and the tautologies. The polar extremes would at least remind us of the contrast between sense-data orientations (for descriptions) and system-orientations which characterize tautologies. And there is some convenience to thinking of inferences as closer to descriptions than to tautologies, and to thinking that our judgments are probably closer to our individual or social criteria (systems) of good or bad, ugly or beautiful, and so on, than to the sense data.

Perhaps a better diagram, however, would be circular:

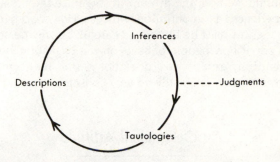

The circular model might serve to remind us that even our statements of description are based on and expressed in words or other symbols, and that these, in turn, are meaningful only as a part of some system. If to this we add arrows suggesting a developmental process they might be such as are expressed in the circular diagram: descriptions leading to inferences in anticipation of the rules of some system, and tautologies which are revised to correspond to new descriptions and new inferences. If such a model is at all useful, we must think of the circular process as continuous and not a single movement around the circle. In our diagram we might also want to leave the category of judgments just outside the circular path which we have described; clearly not all statements of judgment pertain to the mutual dependence and revision of description, inference making, and tautologies.

The scientific method does not deal with statements of judgment as we have presented them. But the other three kinds of statements are the basis of the scientific method. Descriptions of sense data will change, depending on the system in use at the time. What was described by the best science of two hundred years ago in terms of *heat* is now described in terms of *thermodynamics*. Systems will change on the basis of new sense data recorded.[7] The matter of *race* has changed in this century from descriptions of biological data to descriptions of social behavior. The scientific method, the attempt to organize the most scrutinized experiences, is a continuous process. How we organize our own experiences *could* be almost as careful, but my personal inferences about how people behave, on the basis of my own descriptions of my experiences, does not permit me to make the judgment that man is usually so very conscientious.

An Operational Attitude

The concept of *operationalism*, developed both by John Dewey and, especially by the physicist P. W. Bridgman, has made it possible to restrict and test many sentences that previously would have been considered unverifiable. Semanticists have found the concept especially useful, for when one performs a specific operation he is moving from the verbal to the nonverbal level. An operational definition is the instruction for performing some task, the observation of which will explain the concept. If one wants to know what the color *red* is, he may be told to do any of several things in which *red* will appear—"cut your finger and the color of the blood that comes out will be red." Less painful would be the instructions to go to a stoplight and see the color of the light when all of the cars are in line waiting. There are many other possibilities, of course.

Social scientists may operationally define a specific stimulus in an experiment as "anything that causes the rat to jump the grid." Professors may operationally define a *superior student* as

---

[7]Actually, even within the scientific community, systems do not change *solely* on the basis of new sense data recorded. Max Planck has remarked, "A new scientific truth does not triumph by convincing its opponents and making them see the light, but rather because its opponents eventually die, and a new generation grows up that is familiar with it." (Quoted in Max Planck, *Scientific Autobiography and Other Papers* (New York: Gaynor, 1949), p. 33.

anybody who scores over 95 percent correct on a given test. A librarian may operationally define as a *disturbance* anything that makes more than 5 percent of the readers complain that they are unable to read efficiently. In such cases, there is no point in arguing about what a stimulus *really* is, or a superior student *really* is, or a disturbance *really* is. The concept of operationalism assumes the utility of saying "for our purposes." And if one operational definition does not suit the purposes of another individual, he is free to select another operation. Whatever the choice, such an attitude about language has the advantage of agreement through observation.

There is a limitation in the concept of operationalism. If we require all of our statements to be operational before we can trust them or regard them as useful, the value of speculative systems is lost. Often a theory is proposed long before there are ways of making it operational. Indeed, it is the very construction of the theoretical system that opens the ways for new kinds of operations. F. S. C. Northrop has stressed this.

> Again and again in the history of science deductively formulated theories such as Albert Einstein's theory of the finite universe have been constructed as answers to theoretical questions, and at the time of their construction no conceivable operation for testing them was at hand. With further theoretical investigation it often turns out to be possible to derive theorems which do permit the theory to be put to an experimental test. Were all concepts in a scientific theory solely operationally defined concepts, it would be difficult to understand how this could be the case. Then there could be no scientific theory, without the operation for verifying it automatically being present.[8]

Operational definitions can improve many conversations by making more specific some of the loose terms in any kind of sentence and by rendering verifiable statements that would oth-

[8]F. S. C. Northrop, *The Logic of the Sciences and Humanities* (New York: World Publishing Co., 1959, by arrangement with Macmillan), p. 130.

erwise be unverifiable. But where the subject is admittedly speculative, and valuable for that very reason, the criterion of being operational must not be demanded.

Summary

The study of language leads us to an apparent dilemma. On the one hand, we seem to have the freedom to describe the world in many ways; and yet on the other hand, no matter how we describe the world we will be distorting it through our words. We have *abstracted from* and *projected to* that which we wish to describe. *Whatever* we say a thing *is*, it is *not that*.

If you have never thought about this problem before, the realization may be demoralizing. Some students are so shocked that they think they should totally accept nihilism or become mystics or Trappist monks. If one can never speak *truth* one does better to not speak at all. This is one alternative.

But this wears off (usually). Talking is necessary. Often it is fun. And besides, the counterargument goes, we seem to do all right within those limitations. This puts us back to where we started, but with one important difference. Now we are aware of the restrictions and inadequacies of our language, and being thus aware, we will try to be more careful in our speaking and thinking. Some standards within the limitations of language must be established if we are to organize our experiences into meaningful utterances.

In this chapter, we have examined a framework for comparing different kinds of symbolic expressions, a framework limited at one end by statements of immediate sense data, and at the other by statements about some verbal system. Because our language does not directly indicate these different kinds of statements through special symbols, it is important that we be personally critical. Such an awareness may prevent much needless confusion that results from arguing about the use of a word as part of a system as if one were arguing about some verifiable description of sense data.

Statements that report sense data are called *statements of description*, and those that report definitions, rules for usage, and constructs within a system are called *tautologies*. Within these bounds lie *inferential statements*, which rely on both observation and system, and which state a guess about the unknown on the basis of the known. *Value judgments*, a fourth kind of statement, are determined within a personal or cultural system of values. Most sentences cannot be easily classified as just one of these four types unless the conditions that have prompted the statement are also known.

With the application of the operational principle, statements can be related to observable sense data. At these lower levels of abstraction, the chances for understanding and agreement among different persons are greatly increased.

9

When People Talk With People

Words help us to perceive and make sense of the world. Words are also the principal means of sharing with others what we sense and believe and want: Words are our means of communication. But one could overhear a conversation, understand every single word, and completely misunderstand what was said. Understanding interpersonal communication involves at least three considerations, the first of which has traditionally been a part of semantics studies.

In the Domain of Semiotics

You may recall that earlier we discussed the concept of *semiotics*, a name given to a three-part approach to studying symbols: (1) *semantics*—the relationship between symbols and what they represent; (2) *pragmatics*—the relationship between symbols and human responses to them; and (3) *syntactics*—the relationships possible within a system of symbols, such as rules of grammar which vary from language to language.

In this book we have primarily been concerned with the first of these two, largely regarding *meaning* as something to be determined through our every day language habits and responses to words. In the semiotic scheme, we have interpreted *semantics* in terms of *pragmatics*. Syntactics for many years has been the mainstay of linguistics. We have said little about grammatical rules apart from our excursion into the theories of linguistic relativism in Chapter 4, but obviously grammer is a part of meaning. An important part of the grammar of English, for example, is word order; just altering that order slightly can change the meaning of sentence. What's harder than getting a pregnant elephant in a Volkswagon? Getting an elephant pregnant in a Volkswagon.

The semiotics of what is talked about is usually regarded as the subject or the content of communication. It is not, however, the whole of the meaning that we communicate.

Interpersonal Relationships

Important as the semiotic issues are, we cannot understand meaning in conversations between people without some consideration of interpersonal relationships. Consider the following exchange:

A: *What time is it?*
B: *It's one o'clock.*
A: *Thank you.*

We have no knowledge of who A and B might be—they might be intimate friends or total strangers. On the surface, this is an unremarkable exchange where the first person seeks information, the other gives it, and the first person expresses appreciation.

As we will see later in this chapter we could consider possible motives in order to better understand the larger meaning of that exchange. Perhaps it is that A and B are strangers seated next to each other on a plane, and A feels uncomfortable with the silence and breaks it by asking an innocuous question. If this was on A's mind, then the intended meaning would not be the gaining of information but the gaining of a partner for conversation. (See the discussion of "Phatic Communion" elsewhere in this chapter.) To offer that possible interpretation is to raise the issue of interpersonal relationships. The same words expressed in different relationships have different meanings. Until one has some idea of the relationship, the most precise meaning will not be clear.

It is also the case that different relationships will be reflected, some might say defined, the words exchanged. Consider this exchange:

A: *What time is it?*
B. *It's one o'clock.*
A: *Very good!*[1]

In this exchange we can guess with fairly high probability that either A has an odd sense of humor and is playing a joke on B, or A is an elementary school teacher and B is a pupil. If the former were the case we would probably take notice of the exchange, but if this occurred between the student and the teacher we probably wouldn't even remember overhearing it. They are talking the way we expect elementary school students and teachers to talk. Suppose, however, that A were the student and B the

---

[1]For more on this example and an elaboration of its significance for understanding what goes on in the classroom, particularly the multicultural classroom, see R.T. McDermott and Shelly Goldman, "Teaching in Multicultural Settings," in *Proceedings of the Conference on Multicultural Education* (Amersfoot, Netherlands, 1982).

teacher. How might we label little A? Undisciplined? Snotty? Something worse, perhaps.

The point is that everything we say to one another actually incudes two things: some semantic *content* of what the sentence seems to be about; and some expression of the particular *relationship* between the people who are talking.

This relationship may be one of conventional roles, such as the usual role of pupil and teacher, or salesperson and customer, and so on. It may include momentary attitudes and feelings about an ongoing relationship, such as being angry or disappointed or especially affectionate, and so on. It may also be a signal to try to redefine a relationship: When Bernie Schwartz tells an employee, "Don't call me 'Mr. Schwartz,' call me 'Bernie,'" he is saying more about their particular relationship than about his preference in names. On the other hand, Mr. Schwartz may be upset if the new, part-time helper from high school calls him 'Bernie.'

In any case, whenever we are looking at the semantics of words we must ask what the words reveal about the relationship between speaker and listener, or how the relationship is influencing the choice of words and how the listener responds to them.

This distinction between the *content* and *relationship* functions of communication was initially written about in a book that has influenced studies of interpersonal communication, *The Pragmatics of Human Communication*, by Watzlawick, Beavin, and Jackson.[2] The authors identify sets of terms which are comparable to a principle, including *report* and *command*—the former being the apparent semantic content, and the latter being the speaker's intent. The analogy to the computer, as they suggest, may also be helpful. The *content* is something like the data fed into a computer; the *relationship* is more like the program that tells the computer how to interpret that data and respond.

[2]Paul Watzlawick, Janet Beavin, and Don Jackson, *Pragmatics of Human Communication* (New York: W.W. Norton, 1967).

Context

There is a third consideration in interpreting the meanings of words exchanged between people. Curiously, this is something that may involve no words and, in fact, may substitute for words expressed. This is the matter of context.

We often use the word *context* to refer to words that surround words. A prominent spokesperson may complain about "being quoted out of context," meaning that without knowing what went before or after the quoted remark, listeners may get the wrong idea of the speaker's intent. It is true that much of what we say, if extracted from its context, may give a different impression from the one intended.

What we mean by context, however, is even broader than words that surround words. Here (in this context!) we mean in particular: meanings that the speaker and listener share by virtue of common past experiences, common knowledge about the subject matter, and the other matters which are assumed and therefore not necessary to put into words; an understanding of the situation, the time, the place, and the significance of the event itself; and, the means by which a message is communicated: in person, by phone, in a typed letter, on a post card, and so forth.

Context includes a great deal, most of which is unspoken. But unless we consider these matters of context, we may easily misunderstand the speaker's words. Indeed, often the context is far more significant than the expressed words, as it may convey most of the meaning.

Good friends can carry on a half-hour conversation without anyone else having much of an idea of what they are talking about, or what is so funny that they burst into laughter. Their meaning is largely contextual. So much is shared that only a word or two taps into a deep reservoir of meanings. This may be one reason why people who are very close sometimes seem to know what the other is thinking even without any words being expressed. It may be telepathy. But it may be that each draws similar meanings from the unspoken based on past events.

Similarly, in ritual events (discussed in more detail later in this chapter), the meaning of what is said or sung is often very far removed from the particular words that are said or sung. The meaning lies in the past shared experiences of those who participate, and in the associations of certain things being said or done at a particular time and place, but not primarily in the words. What is the meaning of the national anthem or a Christmas carol or Auld Lang Syne sung at New Years? What is the meaning of a wedding vow or the pronouncement of the college president to graduating students at commencement? The meanings are best explored in the area of context, not in the expressed words.

The importance of context in understanding how people communicate and share meaning has been given a prominent place in the work of linguists and anthropologists. You may recall (Chapter 4) that how we use our language, no less than the particular language spoken, may influence how we think about ourselves and the world. Anthropologist Edward T. Hall has developed a theory that extends this notion of context to entire cultures and the rules that guide communication.[3] He notes that some cultures, including mainstream, middle-class American culture, value words. We feel comfortable when meaning is expressed, explicitly, in words. We may feel that if something hasn't been said, then it hasn't been communicated. Hall says we are a very ''low-context culture.'' It is certainly true that general semantics studies, with the attention to words, clarity of expression, objectivity, and so on, is a ''low-context'' field of study.

Many cultures, however, do not value putting into words everything that one wants to communicate. The culture may teach its members that it is best to understand without having to be told, that it is better to learn through observation and sensing the environment, rather than learning through verbal teaching.

[3]Edward T. Hall, *Beyond Culture* (Garden City, N.Y.: Doubleday, 1976).

143

In such *high-context* cultures, speech may not be particularly valued or may be seen as taking away something, in the same way that explaining the punch line of a joke takes away something. Or it may be that speaking is valued, but it is the artfulness of the speaking more than the strict semantic content that is important. This brief description characterizes traditional attitudes toward communication with many Asian cultures. It is also a fair description of some traditional attitudes toward speaking and learning that characterizes many native American cultures.

Context also helps us to understand the meanings of words and symbols in different activities and interests. The words of a novel establish a context for the reader; the final words in the book, therefore, derive their meaning almost entirely from what has preceded. When the heroine on the final page says, "Goodbye forever!" we don't know whether to laugh or cry unless we've read the entire book. A set of instructions on how to open a cereal box, on the other hand, assumes very little previous knowledge. The meaning of an opera is not to be found in the libretto (which gives the text) any more than the meaning of a religious service is to be understood by the literal meaning of hymns and prayers. Both are highly contextual, with meanings apparent to the opera fan or the religious participant, but much less to the outside visitor. A news report of, say, the day's closing prices of the New York Stock Exchange is very low in context: what carries almost all of the meaning is the particular price quoted, not who announces it or with what tone of voice, and so on.

Before we consider some of the many meanings of our words that reflect different purposes or functions, we should remind ourselves that how we say the words we speak—whispered or shouted, fast or slow—can also alter the meaning that is communicated.

Years ago, a popular phonograph record produced by Stan Freberg presented a short conversation between two persons, Marsha and John. The conversation began like this:

"John—"

"Marsha . . . "
"John . . . "
"Marsha . . . "
"John . . . "
"Marsha . . . "

(Using the above dialogue as a basis, the clever reader can extrapolate the entire three-minute conversation.)

The printed form does not convey what the recording artists did with only two words. They were able to indicate differences in meaning by speaking the words with varied inflections and in different tones of voice. In fact, so skillful was the performance that several radio stations banned the harmless record from the air as "too suggestive."

The vocal variations on a theme of two words illustrate two simple but very important points about communication: that the spoken word can have many different intended and interpreted meanings depending upon *how* it is said; and that a phrase or even a single word can serve many functions depending upon its context and the way in which it is expressed. The sensitive conversant, the diplomat, the therapist are well aware of the many purposes of communication that any word or phrase may serve, and yet this awareness is frequently ignored when persons give too much attention to conventional semantics of word-thing relationships. Without such an awareness we must either disregard much, perhaps most, of everyday conversation, or we are likely to totally misinterpret the meaning of all that talk.

Paralanguage

Leo Rosten in his delightful book, *The Joys of Yiddish*[4] suggests that part of the richness of Yiddish lies in the many meanings

[4]Leo Rosten, *The Joys of Yiddish* (London: Penguin Books, 1968).

of some words as determined by a "Yiddish tone of voice." He tells the story of a Russian man who received a telegram from his wife which read: DOCTOR SAYS OPERATE OPERATE. The husband then cabled back immediately this telegram: DOCTOR SAYS OPERATE OPERATE. This exchange aroused the suspicions of the authorities, who immediately invesitgated to see if this was some secret code. But the husband protested that the authorities were misreading the telegram. Clearly what the wife said was: "Doctor says operate. *Operate?*" And the reply: "Doctor says operate, *operate!*"

The general name given to meaningful differences in tone of voice, inflection, rate, pitch, volume, and so forth is *paralanguage*. In ordinary face-to-face conversation, however, even paralanguage describes only a part of all that is communicated to give particular interpretations (or to suggest particular intentions) to any given expression. The social setting (a cocktail party or a funeral), the vast array of nonverbal cues (facial expression, hair style, clothing, eye behavior, posture, distance between the people conversing, and gestures), and even the difference between what we expect to hear and what we think we hear all render apparently similar reports into apparently different commands. Some writers have called all such aspects different commands. Some writers have called all such aspects of communication *metacommunication*. (We should note that metacommunication is sometimes used with quite different meanings, including the technical language used for analyzing communication).

As mentioned earlier, most of traditional semantic studies and even a large portion of general semantics literature have so stressed the word-thing relationship (the semantic dimension in Morris's three-part scheme) and have relied so much on printed or written words that paralinguistic and functional considerations of meaning have been overlooked. But unless we pay attention to these concerns we will run into the same kind of problem that foreign language students face when they are too literal minded about the language they are studying, reporting one's state of health when asked "How are you?" or, in Japan giving an honest answer to the question, "Where are you going?" Viewed one way, the two questions seem completely different; viewed *functionally*, the two questions mean about the same thing: "Hello."

Phatic Communion

Small talk, uninspired greetings, and idle chatter are among the description of a fundamental type of communication that Bronislaw Malinowski called *phatic communion*. To show that we welcome communication, that we are friendly, or that we at least acknowledge the presence of another person, we exchange words. In English we do not have special words for this function of communication, though phatic communion tends to be rather unimaginative. We say, "How are You?" or "Hello," or "Nice day." There may be variations based on geography ("Howdy!") or familiarity ("Hi ya, Baby!") or specific conditions ("Cold enough for ya?"). Whatever the words, the speaker is saying, in effect, "I see you and I am friendly." The channels of communication are opened.

In phatic communion, the specific words exchanged are not important. This is illustrated in the story of a U.S. businessman who, while traveling to Europe for the first time, finds himself seated across from a Frenchman at lunch. Neither speaks the other's language, but each smiles a greeting. As the wine is served, the Frenchman raises his glass and gesturing to the American says, "*Bon appétit!*" The American does not understand and replies, "Ginzberg." No other words are exchanged at lunch. That evening at dinner, the two again sit at the same table and again the Frenchman greets the American with the wine, saying "*Bon appéetit!*" to which the American replies "Ginzberg." The waiter notices this peculiar exchange and, after dinner, calls the American aside to explain that "the Frenchman is not giving his name—he is wishing you a good appetite; he is saying that he hopes

147

you enjoy your meal." The following day the American seeks out the Frenchman at lunch, wishing to correct his error. At the first opportunity the American raises his glass and says, "Bon appétit!" To which the Frenchman proudly replies, "Ginzberg."

Although in this story the ignorance of a common language made more significant communication impossible, it was the exchange of simple words like Bon appétit (and Ginzberg) that broke the tension of silence and expressed friendship. Without the small talk first there can be no "big talk" later.

The only rule that seems to apply to phatic communion is that the subject of the communication be such that each party can say something about it. That is why everybody talks about the weather. The important thing is to talk—and this is why so much of phatic communion begins with a question, for a question requires a reply.

We do not request specific information in phatic communion and we are not expected to reply with precision or accuracy. If we are greeted with a "How are you?" we do not reply as we might if our doctor asked the question. When we are precise the result is likely to be humorous as when James Thurber was once asked, "How's your wife?" and replied, "Compared to what?"

Specific information is sought in one kind of greeting, however. Members of secret organizations sometimes speak in code when they meet to determine whether each knows the password, special handshake, or other symbol. If the answer to the secret question is not precise, then the other is not regarded as a brother Mason or sister Thetá or whatever, and subsequent communication will be prevented. Such coded phatic communion dates from times when members of such organizations might be persecuted if discovered. Among some "secret organizations" today, the reverse seems to be true. The coded greeting is often expressed loudly, more for the benefit of the outsiders than for the "secret" members. Phatic communion is usually the most casual, even careless, form of communication. The stories of persons passing through receiving lines and saying something like "I just killed my mother-in-law," which is met with a smile and a "Fine,

148

I hope you're enjoying yourself" are well known. They illustrate what little significance is attached to phatic communion, so little that the speaker is not even listened to. In such extreme cases, however, we may wonder to what extent the channels of communication have been opened after that exchange of noises. In any case, it seems that we prefer some noise to no noise.

Blocking of Communication

A second function of communication is the opposite of the first. Just as we rarely open a conversation with "I see you and I am friendly," when this may be the real message of our greeting, we rarely prevent further communication by saying directly, "I don't want to talk to you anymore." This is said sometimes, to be sure. But there are more sophisticated ways that we have mastered.

There are the dismissal reactions "Ha!" "That's crazy!" "Yeah, I'll bet!" and so forth. Whether the speaker intends these to block communication or whether they merely function in this way is often difficult to determine. In either case it takes but a few well chosen reactions to end a conversation—and a few more to end a friendship.

Then there are the guarded utterances or verbal grunts that seem to show a lack of interest in speaker or subject: "Oh, really?" "I see—," "Indeed," or "Hmm."

These brief snips of uninterested responses will end a conversation, and often large hunks of verbiage will achieve the same end. Either the language seems to say nothing or it is so difficult to decipher that it does not seem worth the effort. A favorite technique of naughty children, students taking examinations, and some U.S. Senators is to talk on and on about anything irrelevant to the subject at hand.

149

Recording—Transmitting Functions

One definition of teaching goes something like this: "Teaching is the transmission of the professor's notes into the students' notebooks without their having passed through the mind of either." A few years ago it was reported that a professor at a large Midwestern college put his lectures on tape and had the tape recorder sent into the his classroom and played every day. Weeks later, when he stopped into the room to see if all was going well, he found, on each student's desk, another machine recording the lectures. Allowing for hyperboles this story illustrates a basic function of communication, where the individual performs like a precise and self-contained transmitting and recording machine.

In one sense, all communication is a process of transmitting some information that is received by another. This is one definition of communication. But as we note the variety of ways in which we can describe the kind and purpose of a message sent, the category of transmitting—recording seems insufficient. The category is useful only for the most neutral exchanges of information, messages without intent to be instrumental, compliment the listener, let off steam, and so on. Thus, asking when the next bus leaves and being told; asking what time it is, and being told; reporting or hearing the news, weather, classroom lectures, and so on, all might be examples of this function of communication.

Instrumental Communication

When we say something and something happens as the result of our speaking, our comments have been instrumental in causing that event to happen. The instrumental function of communication is one of its most common purposes. We request a secretary to type three copies of a letter. We ask a friend at dinner to pass the butter. We order a salesman out of the house.

The category of instrumental communication is loose enough to allow for several kinds of statements. There are statments that are clearly instrumental in their wording, for which the result correlates with the language. If we say, "Shut the door" and the door is then shut, we may assume that the noise we made was influential in the shutting of the door. There are also statements for which the results cannot be so easily attributed to our utterances. If on a day planned for a picnic it is raining and we sing, "Rain, rain go away"—and the rain does stop—it would be immodest to assume that our words caused the action. Much of prayer has been traditionally instrumental, and if the faithful believe that some prayers "have been answered," we could say that for these people the prayer was an instrumental communication. We will touch on this subject again when we discuss ritual and the magic function of communication.

Some statements are instrumental in intent or effect, but are not phrased as such. For example, if you want the salt passed to you, you may request it directly (instrumental) or you might comment that the food needs salt (transmitting information). If a wife wants a new fur coat, she may request it directly or she may comment on how well dressed her husband seems, especially when compared to her (apparently an effective technique). One instrumental request may result in a different instrumental action, as when commercial airlines do not ask passengers to stop smoking but to "observe the no smoking sign."

One characteristic of some instrumental statements is a faint resemblance between manner of speaking and the requested action itself. One sometimes speaks as if words *were* instruments, as a belaying pin or rawhide whip are instruments. The voice (see metacommunication) does its best to imitate the desired action, as do voices instrumentally cheering at a football game: "Push 'em back, push 'em back, w-a-a-a-a-y back!"

151

Affective Communication

Communication in which the message is the emotional feelings of the speaker toward a listener is known as *affective communication*. Compliments, praise and flattery, and also snide and cutting remarks may be so classified.

There are affective elements in many of the functions of communication. Phatic communion may contain praise, as when old friends greet by saying, "You're looking great!" As noted in the previous section, instrumental purposes are often best served through affective communication, too.

It has been part of the woman's traditional role in our society to use more affective communication than do men. Where tradition has not given women sufficient power, women have had to achieve their goals indirectly. And this indirection may be reflected in instrumental desires disguised in affective language.

The nonaffective language of fact and description or the language of clear and explicit requests need not be any more desirable than that which is common in interpersonal communications. We admire and respect the clarity of the scientist in writing his report, but we may find him or her less explicit during courtship. Perhaps the reason is that whereas the scientist communicates to others pursuing one goal, the diplomats or the lovers may not be sure they are pursuing the same goal.

Affective language is also *convincing* language. In many cases a person would not do something if asked to do it directly; he would be too aware of reasons that he might not be able to accept. We seem to prefer to do things we think we want to do, not things we are told to do. There is a story of an experiment performed by a university class on its professor. The class set out as a group to apply simple learning theory (reward-punishment) on the professor in order to force him to do something he would not ordinarily do and certainly not do if requested. The emotional rewards and punishments, though nonverbal in this case, are comparable to the use of affective language for instrumental purposes. The class decided it would try to move the professor into a corner from which he would deliver his lectures. The reinforcement was of the kind professors like best, interested expressions on student faces, passionate note taking at his every word, smiles at his whimsy and laughter at his wit. These responses, when appropriate, were made whenever the professor moved in the direction of the desired corner. When he moved in the other direction the class responded with looks of boredom, gazing out the windows, shuffing of feet, and the other academic behaviors one has rehearsed since childhood. By the end of the semester the professor was, indeed giving his lectures from the corner of the room.

Although this story may be apocryphal, affective communication in a variety of situations does move the listener in a way that direct requests would not. The salesman knows it ("I'll make a special deal just for you"), the professor knows it ("I'm sure that your studies of Artaud and Beckett have led you to ask . . ."), the lover knows it. Most persons recognize the influence of words on the ego. ("I'm sure that *you*, dear reader, are very sensitive to the communication process.") To make another person feel good (or bad) through language is a rather common and vital function of communication.

It is possible to characterize attitudes of speakers toward their listeners on the basis of instrumental-affective content. One unpublished study of Mexican attitudes toward male and female members of the Holy Family discovered that the language used toward male statues in a church was almost entirely instrumental in content, whereas the language used before the statue of the Virgin was highly affective[5] This distinction mirrored the differences in language used by children toward their parents in the average Mexican home. It is possible that degrees of anger, hostility, authority, and so on, can be measured by the comparitive

---

[5]Cynthia Nelson, "Saints and Sinners: Parallels in the Sex-Role Differentiation in the Family of Saints and in the Family of Man in a Mexican Peasant Village" (mimeographed, N.D.).

content of instrumental and affective language in our everyday expressions.

Many criticisms of the United States visitor or resident abroad have their basis in a lack of affective communication and a preponderance of instrumental communication. As a pragmatic people, we may have a cultural tendency to "get down to business," to be impersonal. A former Secretary of State is often quoted in Latin America as having said with some pride that "the United States does not have friends; it has interests." If others are treated as *interests* when they are more accustomed to being treated as brothers or cousins, surely they will resent the change. The nonaffective communication may be honest, fair, sincere. But to one who does not expect it, the communication is cold, unfeeling, mechanical.

"Better understanding through communication" is a popular slogan. Too often what is meant is an improvement in semantics, an increase in the clarity of what we *mean*. We must not forget the affective aspects of communication, and must strive for an increase in the interpersonal attraction that we *feel*.

Catharsis

When you are angry or disturbed or hurt, physically or mentally, you probably give expression to your feelings. It is curious that expressions, which could be as personal as the feelings that evoke them, are rather stylized and predictable within a language. Words like *ouch*! or *oh*! are spoken by a people who speak English, whereas our neighbors who speak Spanish will say *ay*! when they express a comparable feeling. Grunts may be the only universal expression of catharsis.

When pain or frustration is sufficient, our cathartic expression becomes more obviously symbolic. We move from the *ouch*! to words that might be used in other ways, most often words that are socially disapproved of. We swear or curse or substitute words that sound something like the popular curses we long ago learned were *adult* and special. We find that different kinds of expressions for releasing tension are appropriate among different ages and occupations. A sailor who is angry is not expected to say "Oh, goodness me!" and an angry nun is not expected to sound like a sailor.

The physical stimulus finds expression in a symbol. This symbol eventually ceases to stand for, directly, anything in the outside world except an attitude toward whatever produced it. We move from physical sensation to verbal assault on that sensation ("damn it!") in order to achieve release of tension.

The idea of cursing a situation dates to times when the belief in magic language was more common. There was a time when "God damn you" was meant as a magic curse to bring about suffering. The transference into such symbols was a step above the infantile reaction of actually attacking the offending person or object. Children may be observed to run into a wall and then physically retaliate against the wall, kicking it and saying, "You mean old wall." But when the child's father runs into the wall and says "damn it!" (or, if the child is there, "darn it!") he probably is not talking to the wall. He is simply relieving his tension in symbols that have long evolved from their literal meaning.

Because expressions of catharsis have no referential meaning, any word may serve the cathartic function. Probably each person has some favorite expressions for releasing anger. If you were to prepare a list of cathartic expressions, ranking them according to the degree of tension to be released, you might find there are personal favorites for a hierarchy of catharsis. The meaning of any of these expressions is to be found in what they do for us, not in a dictionary nor in what they do for anybody else. Through repetition we give our select swear words added significance, so that with each new experience and repeated expression we may recall the release of tension from past experiences.

If you have studied another language, you may have learned the kinds of swear words that are most common in that language. In the literal translation they may not seem to do much for you.

Obviously, they cannot, for they have not yet come to be associated with the experiences that give them meaning. This same observation might be made for all words, but the language of catharsis, associated with the strongest of emotions, is the most extreme example of the general principle.

Magic[6]

The belief in the magic power of words exists in all cultures and takes the form of superstitions, instrumental curses, aspects of most religions, and minor forms of wishful thinking. At the root of the attitude is the assumption that words are part of the thing to which they refer and, often, that words precede the *thing* (such as expressed in the Bible, "In the beginning was the Word"). Another quality of this attitude is that words "stand for things" in the sense that a friend "stands for" a bride or groom in a marriage by proxy. With this belief it follows that one can alter a thing by altering its word. If I write your name on a piece of paper and burn it, you, too, will burn, or at least suffer pain. Words, in the magical interpretation, must be treated with the same care as one would treat what the words stand for.

A common example of the belief in word-magic is the hesitancy to speak of possible dangers. If, on an airplane, you remark about the possibility of crashing, fellow passengers may turn on you as if your utterance of the possibility might just cause that to happen. In some cases, of course, it may be simply that others

[6]Susanne Langer includes the magic function of language as part of *ritual*. She writes, "Magic . . . is not as method, but a language; it is part and parcel of that greater phenomenon, ritual, which is the language of religion." (*Philosophy in a New Key* [Cambridge, MA.: Harvard University Press, 1942], p. 39.) Although this may have a historical basis and although magic and ritual are also clearly related today, I find it useful to make a distinction between the two.

do not wish to think of unpleasant things; but the manner and intensity of the reply often indicates a very real fear of the words. If the belief in a magic function of communication seems irrational, ask yourself whether in a plane, you ever avoided such thoughts or whether you ever thought, "We will not crash, we will not crash." For better or for worse, the belief that thinking or saying words will have some effect on what the words stand for is an example of the magic function of communication.

In many religions the magic function of language is still present. One would expect this of any institution that is centuries old and seeks to conserve the language and ritual of the past. The distinction between transubstantiation and consubstantiation of the Roman Catholic and Protestant sects is, in part, the difference in attitude toward the magic function of language. Do the bread and wine *become* the body and blood of Christ, or do they merely *symbolize* the body and blood? There are other examples in religions. The Anglican and Roman Catholic faiths retain rituals for the exorcising of spirits from a haunted house. One may wish to make a distinction between these examples and examples of words that call for the intercession of a divine spirit (such as prayers of petition) where the effect is produced not by the utterance of the words but by the action upon the words by another being. The difference is the difference between Ali Baba saying, "Open Sesame!" (and having the cave door open because of the magic in the words) and having the words heard by a god who then opens the door. In the latter case we have an example of instrumental communication[7]

Symbols associated with persons have long been recognized for their magical associations. Personal names have been regarded as "part of the person," so that what is done to the name affects the person in a similar way. (Elements of this attitude are still very common today, as when parents give their child the name of somebody important to them so that the child becomes a namesake.) The magical attitude toward personal names re-

---

[7]Some students are unimpressed by the distinction.

quires that these names not be taken in vain or, in some cases, not even uttered:

> Here the name is never a mere symbol, but is part of the personal property of its bearer; property which is exclusively and jealously reserved to him ... George von der Gabelentz, in his book on the science of language, mentions the edict of Chinese emperor of the third century B.C. whereby a pronoun in the first person, that had been legitimately in popular use, was henceforth reserved to him along ... It is said of the Eskimos that for them man consists of three elements—body, soul, and name. And in Egypt, too, we find a similar conception, for there the physical body of man was thought to be accompanied, on the one hand by his Ka, or double, and on the other, by his name, as a sort of spiritual double ... Under Roman law a slave had no legal name, because he could not function as a legal person.[8]

Cassirer points out, too, that this attitude toward personal names was held by the early Christians, and hence today Christians still say, "In Jesus' name" instead of "In Christ."

The belief in the magic function of language is based on assumptions that are quite opposed to the discipline of semantics, which regards words as a conventional and convenient and without necessary associations to persons or objects in themselves. There is a sense, however, in which words do have *power*. Words have the power to limit our thought, for example, though this is a different sense of the word *power*. With rumor, with labels that evoke signal reactions, and with labels we try to live up to, we see some effects of the power of words. Such powers, however, are not magical, for they are not to be found *in* the words. Rather, the powers are social, and thus they are effective only to the degree that we accept our language without evaluation and respond to words without evaluation. When we understand and

[8]Ernst Cassier, *Language and Myth* (New York: Dover Publications, N.D.), pp. 50–51.

evaluate our language habits, this social magic spell of words is broken.

Ritual

The scene is a Senate Subcommittee hearingroom. A sixty-year-old convicted murderer, Joseph M. Valachi, calmly reports to the investigators some of the history and methods of the crime organization known as Cosa Nostra. According to the press reports, the witness appeared comfortable throughout his testimony until he described his induction into the organization. Emanuel Perlmutter of the *New York Times* reports:

> Valachi said he had been taken into a large room, where 30 or 35 men were sitting at a long table.
>
> "There was a gun and a knife on the table," Valachi testified. "I sat at the edge. They sat me down next to Maranzaro. I repeated some words in Sicilian after him." . . .
>
> "You live by the gun and knife, and die by the gun and knife." . . .
>
> The witness said Maranzaro had then given him a piece of paper that was set afire in his hand.
>
> "I repeated in Sicilian, 'This is the way I burn if I betray the organization.' " . . .
>
> Valachi said the men at the table then "threw out a number," with each man holding up any number of fingers from one to five. The total was taken. Starting with Maranzaro, the sum was then counted off around the table. The man on whom the final number fell was designated as Valachi's *god-father* in the family. Valachi said the lot had fallen to Bonanno.
>
> The witness said that he had then had his finger pricked by a needle held by Bonanno to show he was united to Bonanno by blood. Afterward, Valachi continued, all those present joined hands in a bond to the organization.
>
> Valachi said he was given two rules in Cosa Nostra that

night—one concerning allegiance to it and another a promise not to possess another member's wife, sister or daughter.

For the first time, the witness grew grim. "This is the worst thing I can do, to tell about the ceremony," he said. "This is my doom, telling it to you and the press."[9]

If the ceremoney Valachi described seems strange to us, stranger still is the fear of his doom caused by revealing that secret. For a tough-minded criminal who reported that for him "killing was like breathing," who gave evidence about the methods and men of the Cosa Nostra, why should the most fearful disclosure be his report of some remote and grisly rite performed years ago? The answer to that question is part of the answer to why some rituals affect almost all of us.

Few organizations or institutions have rituals quite like the Cosa Nostra. The language of the rituals of secret organizations, social fraternities, lodges, and some religious or political organizations is kept secret, known only to their members. But the language of other rituals—patriotic, religious, academic, and so on—is not kept private. Nevertheless, an oath of allegiance or a communal prayer can affect the nervous system as no statement of fact or judgment can.

Ritual is sometimes described as the behavioral part of a mythology. The mythology may be for almost any purpose, but consistently it emphasizes a sense of community among its members and a sense of permanence. To participate in a ritual is to participate in a community, often one that claims a tradition of centuries. The sense of timelessness is quite important. When the anthropologist asks the primitive why he performs a certain ritual, the answer might be, "because our ancestors have always done this." If in the modern-day United States our sense of tradition is a short one, we may find the same comfort in rituals

---

[9]Emanuel Perlmutter, "Valachi Names 5 as Crime Chiefs in New York Area," *New York Times*, October 2, 1963, p. 28.

realizing that we as individuals have always said the pledge or sung the hymn.

Comparatively speaking, the United States has never been overly enthusiastic about most rituals; many of our most important cultural values conflict with the values of ritual. Ritual celebrates permanence, while the United States values change; rituals celebrate the community, while Americans extoll individualism and "going it alone." Ritual is rooted in the past, while Americans are more concerned with the future. Nevertheless there has been a rise in the ritual function of communication for at least a sizable portion of the American public, particularly among the younger members. Indeed, part of what has come to be celebrated in some rituals might be considered as *youth*. Another part of the ritual function has been to celebrate a youthful community as distinct from *the older generation, the establishment, the straight people*, or whatever the outsiders happened to be called. In dress and hair styles, certainly in language and in music, in rallying figures (most notably among rock musicians), a kind of community is established.

There appears to be little that is instrumental in the performance of a ritual, with some notable exceptions. Sociologist Robert Merton has noted that activities originally conceived as instrumental often become transmuted into ends in themselves. What was originally obtained through certain words or acts is no longer needed or desired. If at one time meat had to be prepared in a certain way to avoid contamination, meat may still be prepared in such a way because "that's the way our ancestors did it." If certain prayers were recited with the hope of rewards, the same prayers may be repeated even though a congregation no longer expects those rewards. In many, perhaps most, cases, a new mythology will develop to explain certain words and actions of a ritual. It is not clear whether rituals continue to exist by virtue of constant repetition or whether the participants in a ritual feel that some ends are being served.

Three characteristics of most rituals are most important. The rituals must be performed with others (immediately or symbolically present); they must be performed on some occasion; and they must be performed with special care to details.

This last characteristic makes ritual somewhat different from other forms of communication. Many children have difficulty with the high-level abstractions and archaic language often present in ritual. The usual vocabulary of children contains few high-level abstractions. But a child will learn to imitate or approximate the sounds of the rituals in which he finds himself participating. Frequently these words become translated in his own vocabulary without conflict. My niece and nephew, when very young, sang their favorite Christmas carol in church. The boy concluded "Silent Night" with the words "Sleep in heavenly beans." "No," his sister corrected, "not beans, peas."

Most of us have associations with aspects of some rituals from our earliest memories. Perhaps you have had the sudden awareness of what some words you have been saying all your life were really supposed to be. It can be both a startling and amusing realization. But it is one that characterizes a form of communication in which repetition of certain words over an expanse of time is most important.

For some persons, part of the appeal of ritual may be the pleasure of solemnly repeating words that seem to have no referent; this may evoke a mood of mystery for such persons. Other persons may find a deep satisfaction in discovering the meaning of what they have been saying for years. Such attitudes, if they exist, would seem to be unhealthy, not only as regards an understanding of the purpose of language but also for the significance of the ritual itself.

There are other characteristics of ritual that make it distinct from other functions of language in communication. One of these is the sublimation function of ritual. Through ritual, a person may symbolically take part in an event that would exclude his actual participation. During wartime, rituals tend to become more common and more significant. The displaying of the flag, the reciting of the pledge of allegiance, even the rationing of food and gasoline are ways of symbolically participating in the war effort. Or, to take a happier example, during a football game the fans who wish to help their team may better do so by cheering than by assisting on the field. It is common, for example, that at the kick-off the fans will shout together, as if their noise will help to carry the ball farther down field.

Some rituals last longer than their mythologies. At the time when some persons begin to question religious beliefs, they may find it relatively easier to "lose the faith" than to lose the habit of prayer or church attendance on certain holy days. A sense of compulsiveness frequently attends ritual, and a sense of guilt may enter when ritual has gone. As a nation becomes what is called a *nontraditional society*" the rituals that are a part of the tradition die. This finds expression as *alienation*. It may also explain, in part, the attraction for many philosophies of the *absurd*. If a society's stability has been largely dependent on ritual and the rituals fall, it is an easy out to label the world *absurd*.

Conventions of many kinds, political, social, and academic often serve more of a ritual function than the function of exchanging information or achieving some instrumental goal. To see the partcipants cheer or clap as the speaker speaks the holy jargon and drops the right names at the right time is amusing and a little sad at the same time. What is called a report may better serve as an incantation. No group can maintain itself without strong cohesiveness, it is true. But if the main result of the group's effort is only cohesiveness, then surely we have the origins of a new ritual.

On Saying What You Mean and Meaning What You Say

Semanticists are sometimes thought to desire complete honesty of expression, directness, and "no beating around the bush." An understanding of the many purposes of communication should dispel that view. We use language for too many purposes and find ourselves forced to make some comment in too many difficult situations to hold a such a goal. Simple friendship, not to mention diplomacy and tact, prohibits us from always saying what we are thinking.

Suppose, for example, some friends are in a play. You attend the opening-night performance, which is, as accurately as you can judge it, a real turkey. Then, as you leave the theater, you encounter your friends and the director. Do you say what you are thinking and maybe hurt a friendship? Do you betray your critical integrity? No. Assuming that you cannot avoid comment, you equivocate, you speak in ambiguities. The popular expressions for this moment of untruth are many: "Well, you've done it again!" (to the director); "You should have been in the audience!" (to the actors); "It was an unforgettable evening!" (to the elderly bystander who may be the dean, the director's father, or the play-wright).

If you feel that the potential ridicule of these expressions is too strong, you may equivocate further with the always safe "Congratulations!"

One may protest that these comments, however deft, are nonetheless lies and should not be excused. I think, however, that to regard them so is to confuse standards of different functions of communication. Affective communication directed to the emotional responses of the listener does not require the accuracy, even of judgments, that the transmission of specific information does. The purpose is often friendship, not a critical evaluation. Often it is much more important to tell a person that you like his tie, coat, smile, voice, and so on, than to be bound by some standards of judgment which would severely limit your affective communications. A kind or friendly remark often does more for human understanding than a diplomatic silence or a hundred "honest" judgments.

To be aware of the many functions of communication is to be alive and sensitive to the most basic of human needs. As our needs for bodily health and comfort are met, we become more aware of (and create new) needs for symbolic health and comfort. To be loved or respected, to help others, to feel trust—the list could be elaborated greatly—becomes extremely important. Each communication situation both reveals our frailty and offers some promise for support.

Recommended Reading

Allport, Floyd H. *Theories of Perception and the Concept of Structure*. New York: John Wiley and Sons, 1955.

Berger, Peter and Thomas Luckman. *The Social Construction of Reality*. Garden City: Doubleday Anchor, 1966.

Bernstein, Basil. *Class, Codes and Control*. New York: Shocken Books, 1975.

Birdwhistell, Ray. L. *Kinesics and Context*. Philadelphia: Univ. of Pennsylvania Press, 1971.

deBono, Edward, *Lateral Thinking*. New York: Harper & Row, 1970.

Bollinger, Dwight, *Aspects of Language*, Second Ed. New York: Harcourt, Brace Jovanovich, 1975.

Bois, Samuel. *Explorations in Awareness*. New York: Harper & Row. 1957.

Bronowski, J. *Science and Human Values*. Baltimore: Penquin Books, 1964.

Brown, Roger. *Words and Things*. Glencoe: The Free Press, 1958.

Burke, Kenneth. *A Grammar of Motives*. New York: Prentice-Hall, 1955.

———. *A Philosophy of Literary Form*. New York: Prentice-Hall, 1941.

Carroll, John. *The Study of Language*. Cambridge: Harvard Univ. Press, 1953.

Cassirer, Ernst. *Language and Myth*. New York: Harper & Row, 1946.

Chase, Stuart. *The Power of Words*. New York: Harcourt Brace Jovanovich, 1954.

Condon, John. A *Bibliography of General Semantics*. (Originally published by ETC.: A *Review of General Semantics* in five installments; available from the International Society for General Semantics.)

———— and Fathi Yousef. *Intercultural Communication*. Indianapolis: Bobbs-Merrill, 1974.

ETC.: A *Review of General Semantics*. (published quarterly)

Goodstein, R. L., "Language and Experience," in Arthur Danto and Sidney Morgenbesser (eds.) *Philosophy of Science*. New York: World Publishing Co., 1959, p. 1–132.

Gorman, Margaret. *The Educational Implications of the Theory of Meaning and Symbolism of General Semantics*. Washington, D.C.: The Catholic Univ. of America Press, 1958.

Hall, Edward T. *Beyond Culture*. New York: Doubleday, 1976.

Hastorf, Albert H. and Hadley Cantril, "They Saw A Game: A Case Study," *The Journal of Abnormal and Social Psychology* 49 (January, 1954) (Reprinted as Bobbs-Merrill Reprint in the Social Sciences, Number P-147.)

Hayakawa, S. I. (ed.) *Language, Meaning and Maturity*. New York: Harper & Row, 1954.

————, *Language in Thought and Action*. Second Edition, New York: Harcourt Brace Jovanovich, 1964.

————(ed.) *Our Language and Our World*. New York: Harper & Row, 1959.

————. *Symbol, Status, and Personality*. New York: Harcourt Brace Jovanovich, 1963.

Heinlein, Robert. *A Stranger in a Strange Land*. Berkeley: Berkeley Medalian Books, 1961. (A science fiction novel.)

Henle, Paul (ed.). *Language, Thought and Culture*. Ann Arbor: Ann Arbor Paperbacks, 1965.

Holton, Gerald (ed.) *Science and Culture*, Boston: Beacon Press, 1967.

Johnson, Wendell. *Your Most Enchanted Listener*. New York: Harper & Row, 1956.

Korzybski, Alfred. *Science and Sanity: An Introduction to Non-Aristotelian Systems and General Semantics*. Lancaster, Penn.: Science Press Printing Co., 1933.

————. *Selections from Science and Sanity*. Compiled and arranged by Guthrie Janssen. Lakeville, Conn.: Institute of General Semantics, 1947.

Kuhn, Thomas S. *The Structure of Scientific Revolutions*, Second Ed., Enlarged. Chicago: University of Chicago Press, 1970.

Lakoff, George and Mark Johnson, *Metaphors We Live By*. Chicago: University of Chicago Press, 1980.

Langer, Susanne K. *Philosophy in a New Key*. Cambridge: Harvard Univ. Press, 1942.

Lee, Dorothy. *Freedom and Culture*. Englewood Cliffs, N.J.: Prentice-Hall, 1959.

Lee, Irving. *Customs and Crises in Communication*. New York: Harper & Row, 1954.

————. *The Language of Wisdom and Folly*. New York: Harper & Row, 1949.

Lenneberg, Eric. *The Biological Foundations of Language*. New York: John Wiley and Sons, 1967.

McKellar, Peter. *Imagination and Thinking: A Psychological Analysis*. New York: Basic Books, 1957.

Miller, Casey and Kate Swift, *Words and Women*. Garden City, N.Y.: Doubleday, 1977.

Miller, George. *Language and Communication*. New York: McGraw-Hill, 1951.

Morris, Charles. *Signs, Language and Behavior*. Englewood Cliffs, N.J.: Prentice-Hall, 1946.

Northrop, F. S. C. *The Logic of the Sciences and the Humanities*. New York: Macmillan, 1947.

Ogden, C. K. and I. A. Richards. *The Meaning of Meaning*, Third Edition Revised. New York: Harcourt Brace Jovanovich, 1930.

Orwell, George. *1984*. London: George Allen, 1948.

Osgood, Charles, George J. Suci, and Percy H. Tannenbaum. *The Measurement of Meaning*. Urbana: University of Illinois Press, 1957.

Papert, Seymour, *Mind-Storms: Children, Computers and Powerful Ideas*. New York: Basic Books, Inc., 1980.

Piaget, Jean. *The Language and Thought of the Child*. New York: Harcourt Brace Jovanovich, 1926.

Popper, Karl R. *The Logic of Scientific Discovery*. New York: Science Editions, 1961.

Rapoport, Anatol. *Fights, Games and Debates*. New York: Harper & Row, 1960.

————. *Operational Philosophy*. New York: Harper & Row, 1953.

Reichenbach, Hans. *The Rise of Scientific Philosophy*. Berkeley: University of California Press, 1959.

Rogers, Carl R. *On Becoming a Person*. Boston: Houghton Mifflin, 1967.

Ruesch, Jurgen. *Therapeutic Communication*. New York: W. W. Norton, 1961.

———— and Gregory Bateson. *Communication: The Social Matrix of Psychiatry*. New York: W. W. Norton, 1951.

Russell, Bertrand. *An Inquiry into Meaning and Truth*. Baltimore: Penquin Books, 1962.

Sapir, Edward. *Language: An Introduction to the Study of Speech*. New York: Harcourt Brace Jovanovich, 1921.

Satir, Virginia. *Conjoint Family Therapy*. Palo Alto: Science Books, 1964.

Shannon, Clyde and Warren Weaver. *The Mathematical Theory of Communication*. Urbana: University of Illinois Press, 1951.

Stewart, Edward C. *American Cultural Patterns: A Cross-Cultural Perspective*. Pittsburgh: Regional Council for International Education, 1971.

Ullmann, Stephen. *Semantics: An Introduction to the Science of Meaning*. New York: Barnes and Noble, 1962.

Von Bertalanffy, Ludwig. *General Systems Theory*. New York: Braziller, 1968.

Watzlawick, Paul. *How Real is Real?* New York: Random House, 1976.

Watzlawick, Paul, Janet Beavin, and Don Jackson. *The Pragmatics of Human Communication*. New York: W. W. Norton, 1967.

Weinberg, Harry. *Levels of Knowing and Existence*. New York: Harper & Row, 1959.

White, Leslie. *The Science of Culture*. New York: Grove Press, 1963.

Whorf, Benjamin Lee. *Language, Thought and Reality: Selected Writings of Benjamin Lee Whorf* (John B. Carroll, ed.) New York: John Wiley and Sons, 1956.

Wiener, Norbert. *The Human Use of Human Beings: Cybernetics and Society*. Boston: Houghton Mifflin, 1950.

Index

171

9980